Intensive Training in Christian Spirituality

Why There Has To Be A

Hell

Gil Stieglitz

Why There Has To Be A Hell

Copyright © Gil Stieglitz 2011

Published by Principles to Live By, Roseville CA 95661
www.ptlb.com

Cover by John Chase

All Rights reserved. No part of this publication may be reproduced, stored in a retrieval system, or transmitted in any way by an means-electronic, mechanical, photocopy, recording, or otherwise-without the prior permission of the copyright holder, except as provided by USA copyright law.

All Scripture verses are from the New American Standard Bible unless otherwise indicated.

New American Standard Bible: 1995 update.

1995 La Habra, CA: The Lockman Foundation.

ISBN 978-0-9909641-6-2

Printed in the United States of America

Dedication

This book is dedicated to
THE LORD GOD ALMIGHTY
who has graciously allowed us a way to escape
the awful confines of Hell through the wondrous life,
death, and resurrection of His only begotten Son,
THE LORD JESUS CHRIST.

Table of Contents

Preface..7

Introduction..9

1. What Does Jesus Tell Us About Hell?....................13

2. The Architecture of Hell......................................39

3. The Future of Hell..59

4. Part I: Why There Has To Be A Hell...................81

5. Part II: Why There Has To Be A Hell.................117

Conclusion..141

End Notes...147

Appendix 1...149

About the Author..161

Other Resources..163

Preface

There may be a temptation to skip the first few chapters of this book and jump to the reasons why there must be a Hell but do not do that. It is important that you work through what Jesus says and grapple with His words. It is His words and His ideas that are full of grace and truth. When you spend enough time with what Jesus says, a different perspective will emerge. You will find yourself ready to receive the truth of hell presented in the other chapters. If you jump to the reasons for hell, then this book will become just one more philosophical discussion or intellectual game on the subject of hell.

When we approach hell or any part of the afterlife without a biblical framework, we place ourselves in the position of judges and authorities over God's constructs and concepts. This is a very troubled position. It is very much like when scientists decided that certain organs in the body were vestigial organs from previous evolutionary generations and declared that these organs could and should be removed.[1] Without a biblical framework and submission to Jesus our wisdom will fail us when we deal with topics like hell.

Things that appear right to us and our limited perspective are pronounced wrong and destructive by God because of His knowledge, wisdom, and infinity. If people presume to place themselves as judges over the existence and attributes of hell, our pride will take over and we will miss key truths God is trying to communicate with us. Hell exists for all eternity whether you want it to exist or not.

No book would be produced without the many people who help make a manuscript complete. Let me thank Sandy Johnson for her tireless efforts to keep my grammar and sentence structure right. Any errors still in the manuscript are mine and not hers. I am indebted to the student ministries of Adventure Christian Church for their helpful critique: David Hopper, College Ministries Director; Brian Haas, High School Ministries Director; David Sauer, Junior High Director. These men provided key insights and help in making the manuscript a much more helpful and complete work. Also my good friend, Gary Basham, who generously took time out of his busy law practice to help me grapple with how to say some of the hard things in this book.

Introduction

Shall not the Judge of all the earth deal justly?
Genesis 18:25

Recently I sat in the living room of a friend. Right in front of me was a hospital bed that had been jammed into the room to accommodate a new reality - my friend was dying. He lay motionless in the last few hours of his life. He was emaciated and radically pale as he labored to breathe as the cancer that had attacked him continued to do its awful work. I wept and prayed with the family as we tried to embrace the reality that had barged into our lives. Their husband, their father, my friend was going to die very soon. Just nine weeks before he was robust and energetic and fully engaged in life. Then he felt a little tired and run down so he took a few days off. He thought he had the flu. His wife argued him into going to the doctor because she thought it might be a little more than the flu. The doctor did the tests and came back with the grim news. "You have acute stage four leukemia, and you have less than six months to live." My friend had been in denial about what was happening in his body. No one develops stage four cancer in two days. Whatever aches and pains he had were most likely attributed to getting older. Whatever lack of energy he experienced was probably chalked up to a lack of sleep. If there was any weight loss in the last six months, it was probably thought to be related to his concern for the future and/or a new diet. But the cancer had been there for awhile. It was working in secret and he was in denial. The cancer had been doing its work for months, building up its reserves, and preparing for its all-out assault on his body. He only truly understood its presence when it launched its final offensive. It took him down in nine weeks. It is scary that we can be in denial about a reality that is as deadly as leukemia. But leukemia is only about the death of the body. There is a much more scary reality that far more people are in denial about.

There is a great game of denial going on in western civilization. We are in denial that we will die. We are in denial that there is conscious existence after death. We are in denial that anyone actually goes to hell. We have substituted a real view of the universe for a completely materialistic and mechanistic understanding of our lives and existence. We have denied the existence of the spirit world and the possibility of life after death. This is in spite of the fact that every society before this modern world affirmed both the spirit world, life after death, and consequences for our choices that extend into and through eternity. As our world has rushed to a mechanistic view of the world, it has stripped meaning, love, ultimate morality, and purpose from our lives. It has also pushed away the idea of consequences for our decisions that extend beyond this life.

We have come to believe that if there is an afterlife, anyone who goes through the pain of transitioning to that other plane of existence will automatically be absolved of their selfish choices and welcomed into heaven. Almost no serious theology sees the afterlife in this way. We are also currently in the business in the west of failing to address the issue of hell because the facts we do have regarding hell do not meet our preconceived ideas of a loving God. But sacred literature does not shy away from teaching facts about the afterlife and the truths regarding the consequences for our choices. This short book is designed to expose biblical truths that should inform our understanding of life, life after death, the love of God, and the consequences of our lives.

Sometimes facts are unpleasant. The forests are being destroyed. Nuclear material used to heat water lasts for millions of years in a toxic state. Thousands of people are maimed and killed each year by drunk drivers. Thousands of men, women, boys, and girls are forced into sex slavery every year. Thousands of animals are abused each year. These are facts.

Christian theology looks at these realities and gives us truth, no matter how unpleasant it is. Christian theology has answers to the big questions of life. Christian theology uses the Bible as its source material. It is in the Bible that we find the answers that we seek for the key questions in life. There are other worldviews out there with their answers. And numerous people invent their own ideas that they like better than the Bible's answers, but Christians are committed to the truths that Scripture gives us.

Let me start by saying that I do not have all the answers. I don't even have all the questions. But I do know that there are certainties in a Christian worldview. God has given us the broad outlines of the truth about our existence here in this world. One of these broad outlines is the existence of hell. There is a heaven to gain and a hell to lose. Here are a few other things I know from the Christian worldview. I do know that it matters how one lives their life. I do know that the choices that we make echo through eternity. I do know that there is a need for justice beyond what is meted out in this world. Sitting with my friend in the last hours of his life and reading my Bible made that clear to me. Heaven is real. Hell is real. The choices we make in this life matter for all eternity. I offer this book as a starter discussion on the reality and reasons for hell.

Chapter 1

What Does Jesus Tell Us About Hell?

There is growing interest in answers to the big questions of life. I applaud any honest searching into these crucial questions.

- Who am I?
- How do we know that we know?
- Are ethics more than an emotional response to abnormal behaviors?
- Why am I here?
- What happens after I die?
- Is there a God?
- How did the world come into existence?
- Is love more than just a biological response?
- What is my purpose?
- What is beauty?
- Is there any meaning to life?
- Why is there so much evil in the world?

- Are our lives more than the predictable natural, outworking of chemical processes and random energy fluctuations of the past?

My own questions and searching have led me to find the answers in Christian theology. Yes, the classic definitions and categories of the Christian faith answer most completely the philosophic and pragmatic questions of life.

All of the above questions -- and many others -- are now bombarding the thinkers of western civilization. The last few hundred year's experiment with naturalistic and materialistic philosophy as the replacement for Christian theology in the west is failing because of its inadequate answers to these key questions. This is especially true in the areas of meaning, purpose, morals, and love.

This book is not meant to be a philosophic discussion of the merits or demerits of life after death or the existence of hell but instead a basic view of Christian theology's teaching on the reality and reasons for hell. I will leave to my more philosophic and theological colleagues to write the other books that will put a finer and deeper point on these matters.

In his excellent book, *The Case for Faith,* Lee Strobel interviews J.P. Moreland about how we should approach any discussion of the afterlife and hell. Let's listen in to these insightful comments:

How should we approach the topic of Hell?

We should distinguish between liking or disliking something and judging whether it is right to do.

The basis of their evaluation should be whether hell is a morally just or morally right state of affairs not whether they like or dislike the concept.[1]

Too often we have been trying to think about whether we like heaven or hell rather than evaluating the data we have on these places.

For the Christian, the Bible -- both Old and New Testament -- is the source material for what we believe about faith and our lives. So our search for understanding the truths about the afterlife must be rooted in the Scriptures and not speculative philosophy. It is possible to speculate about the interpretation and possibilities of the Scriptural data and meaning; but a Christian starts with Scripture, not with what they think the afterlife should be like.

Of all the places to look in Scripture for teaching about the afterlife, it is important to begin by listening to Jesus. He is our supreme teacher. He sees through the clutter of cultural frames and gives us accurate information about the eternal world. He knows and can accurately describe for our limited perspective the truths of the afterlife. This is why it is important to start thinking accurately about the afterlife by listening to Jesus. Jesus has two extended discussions about the afterlife with His disciples. We will look at each of those discussions in this book. We start with Jesus' true account of Lazarus and the rich man. Read through the Scriptural discussion and then begin answering the questions that follow. Then read the paragraphs that follow:

> **Luke 16:19-31 -** *Now there was a rich man, and he habitually dressed in purple and fine linen, joyously living in splendor every day. And a poor man named Lazarus was laid at his gate, covered with sores, and longing to be fed with the crumbs which were falling*

from the rich man's table; besides, even the dogs were coming and licking his sores. Now the poor man died and was carried away by the angels to Abraham's bosom; and the rich man also died and was buried. In Hades he lifted up his eyes, being in torment, and saw Abraham far away and Lazarus in his bosom. And he cried out and said, "Father Abraham, have mercy on me, and send Lazarus so that he may dip the tip of his finger in water and cool off my tongue, for I am in agony in this flame." But Abraham said, "Child, remember that during your life you received your good things, and likewise Lazarus bad things; but now he is being comforted here, and you are in agony. And besides all this, between us and you there is a great chasm fixed, so that those who wish to come over from here to you will not be able, and that none may cross over from there to us." And he said, "Then I beg you, father, that you send him to my father's house— for I have five brothers—in order that he may warn them, so that they will not also come to this place of torment." But Abraham said, "They have Moses and the Prophets; let them hear them." But he said, "No, father Abraham, but if someone goes to them from the dead, they will repent!" But he said to him, "If they do not listen to Moses and the Prophets, they will not be persuaded even if someone rises from the dead."

How does Jesus tell us about hell?

As was Jesus' way, He tells us the truth about life and reality through the use of stories. In this case it seems to be a true story of two different men and their entrance and initial existence in eternity. This does not seem to be a fictional story because of the detail that Jesus gives of the men and the fact that he names the one man.

What Does Jesus Tell Us About Hell?

The two men are described as a rich man and a poor man named Lazarus. The rich man has an overwhelming amount of goods so that he does not need to worry about each day's provisions. The word translated *rich* is the word *plousios*, which means wealthy and abundance of money and goods. In a day and age of day laborers -- where people needed to collect their wages every day in order to have enough to eat that day -- to be wealthy meant that you did not have to worry about your meals or lodging for that day. Remember there were no refrigerators and no grocery stores. Meat would go bad within three days at most unless it was salted and vegetables could not be preserved unless they were pickled. The majority of people did not have any food stored up. So when Jesus says that this man was wealthy, it meant that he had more than enough for himself, his family, and others if he was willing to employ them and share. But as we will see, he was not willing to invest anything in those around him.

The rich man is described as habitually dressing in purple and fine linen. There are three words that are key to the idea Jesus is trying to convey. They are translated: habitually dressing, purple, and fine linen. The word translated, *habitually dressed*, means that this was the custom every day for this man to put on purple garments and fine linen. Remember this was a culture in which most people had one or, at the most, two different changes of clothes -- one suit of clothing for everyday use and a second for dress-up occasions such as synagogue or other social gatherings. This was a man who dressed in different exquisite garments every day. He spoiled himself every day. He did not work but dressed to impress others every day. To wear purple in that day meant that the person was of importance or had authority, as that was a royal color -- a color of authority and power. It was not a naturally occurring color. His wearing of purple every day suggests to Jesus' audience that this person was into impressing others and reminding himself of how important he was. Remember, he did not dress in purple just when he had official business; instead he dressed in purple habitually. This man wanted to remind himself and everyone every day how much power and authority he had. And yet when he was asked to use that power and authority to help someone in desperate need right outside his gate, he did not act. He did not use his authority. Finally Jesus says that he dressed in fine linen. The word is *bussa*, which denotes a very costly Egyptian flax. It was delicate, extremely soft, and white in color. This was not the working person's underwear. It suggested pampering oneself.

Jesus finishes His first description of the rich man with the phrase *joyously living in splendor every day*. The people in Jesus' day would have understood this phrase as indulging himself through the use of his wealth every single day. There was no hard work trying to benefit society in some way. This man's riches were piled up so he could indulge himself from a purely selfish perspective. The man spent his abundance on himself and his own pleasure.

If a person was blessed by God, then they had a responsibility to the larger community. They benefitted from the larger community; therefore, they needed to give back to that community in various forms. It was considered the height of selfishness to spend your abundance on yourself instead of looking to what God may have for you to spend it on. There are a number of examples of people of great wealth in the Old Testament who were very close to God, but none of them spent their wealth on pleasing themselves alone. This was true of Abraham, Isaac, King David, Job, and others. God does give riches but these come with responsibilities. God does not allow a concentration of wealth in your lap for you to spend upon yourself alone or you will be heaping up treasures to your own heart (James 5:1-6). We are to be a river, not a reservoir.

> **James 5:1-6** - *Come now, you rich, weep and howl for your miseries which are coming upon you. Your riches have rotted and your garments have become moth-eaten. Your gold and your silver have rusted; and their rust will be a witness against you and will consume your flesh like fire. It is in the last days that you have stored up your treasure! Behold, the pay of the laborers who mowed your fields, and which has been withheld by you, cries out against you; and the outcry of those who did the harvesting has reached the ears of the Lord of Sabaoth. You have lived luxuriously on the earth and led a life of wanton pleasure; you have fattened your hearts in a day of slaughter. You have condemned and put to death the righteous man; he does not resist you.*

It is entirely possible that this description also suggests that the rich man indulged himself in pleasures beyond clothing, such as immorality. Very similar to what we would call partying. But Jesus does not specify this in his description. He does strongly state that the rich man was self-promoting, self-focused, and self-important. The infection of selfishness had clearly taken hold in this man. His wealth and abundance was not seen as a gift from God for benefiting others. His riches were seen as his to consume in any way he wanted, and he wanted to consume it on himself.

Now remember that rich people in that day were seen as specifically blessed by God. Jesus chooses to talk about hell differently by upending the average person's understanding of who is in which compartments in the afterlife. Most Jews at that time thought that the rich were rich because God was blessing them. They were considered more worthy than other people, which is why

God let them have wealth. The poor were considered to be cursed by the Almighty, which was why this true story about two real men was so powerful. A person who had abundance was understood as being incredibly blessed by God, so for Jesus to talk about a rich person in hell was shocking. It would be like placing Mother Teresa or Billy Graham in hell. Jesus would clearly have people's attention. They would think that if rich people can end up in hell, then anybody could be there. Since Jesus names Lazarus as a real individual, it is possible that some of his hearers knew him and may have even known who the unnamed rich man was. Jesus has their attention and they are riveted on his explanation of Sheol.

WHAT DO WE LEARN ABOUT THE POOR MAN?

We learn six specific things about this poor man:

First, we learn that his name was Lazarus. Jesus' naming of this individual strongly indicates that this is not a fictional story to make a point but rather a real episode about real people entering eternity.

Secondly, Lazarus was a poor man. This word translated poor can be translated beggar, destitute, asking for handouts. He had nothing as visible means of support except the pity of people with abundance. There are hints later that Lazarus was a giving and loving person before he fell sick. If he does not receive aid every day, he will die.

This type of poor person was beyond unemployed: he was not able to care for himself. We would call him significantly and permanently disabled. Lazarus was completely at the mercy of the society at large and individuals who could and should help. Jesus seems to pick this pair to describe because it shows such contrast.

What Does Jesus Tell Us About Hell?

The selfishness of the rich man is so evident. The extreme need of the poor man Lazarus was so undeniable. In that culture it would not be uncommon to have the poor begging. There were no state agencies and governmental programs to help these folks. Remember that it wasn't until Christians founded hospitals, sanitariums, hostels, and relief organizations that these needs were addressed in an organized way.

Third, take notice that Lazarus was laid at the gate of the rich person, which was where the abundance might flow down to him. He did not have the ability to move himself to the gate of the rich man, which suggests that he had some physical disability, or injury which prevented him from walking. Someone who knows him puts him in the best place to get help and he receives none. This cold-heartedness on the part of the rich man would have been shocking to the culture of the time. If God has blessed you, then you must share with those who are less fortunate.

Jesus, fourthly, describes Lazarus as one who was covered with sores. He had unhealed wounds. It is unclear why Jesus mentions this detail. It could be because sickness would have made Lazarus more pitiful or that these sores could have made him appear repulsive. Whatever the case, he was sick, disabled, destitute, and dropped off at the one place where someone could look with pity on him. The rich man, instead, is more interested in pleasing himself and spending his abundance on himself than on his societal obligation to people like Lazarus.

Jesus' fifth detail about Lazarus the poor man is that this man was longing to be fed with the crumbs that were falling from the rich man's table. This detail tells us that Lazarus realized why he had been placed at the rich man's gate and what he was supposed to do. He was supposed to ask for benevolence on the part of the rich man. The fact that he was longing for this little pittance from the rich man suggests that he waited in vain for the rich man's mercy. The rich man was too busy spending his abundance on himself to hear the poor man at his gate. Now remember that this was the day when no one had cars and garages to cocoon themselves. In order for the rich man to conduct business and live his life, he would have to walk out the gate and see Lazarus lying there and hear him beg for crumbs. We know that the rich man knows Lazarus because he calls him by name later in the story.

The final detail Jesus uses to show the condition of Lazarus is he lets us know that even the dogs were coming and licking his sores. Dogs were not cute cuddly pets but dirty, mangy scavengers. In that culture they were seen like we see cockroaches. They were to be avoided. Lazarus does not have the energy or ability to drive the dogs away. This is a person who is unable to move except to beg and is covered with sores in which the cockroaches are his only medical attendants. If there ever was a person for whom the rich man should have been struck with pity and mercy, it should have been Lazarus. But, no, the rich man is completely self-focused, self-absorbed, and self-important.

How did the two men enter into the afterlife?

With these details, Jesus now begins the action of these two men entering into eternity. Jesus has his audience because of the sympathy they feel for the poor man and the typical perceived blessing of God on the rich man. Jesus tells us three crucial details about the poor man's entrance into heaven.

First, he tells us that the man died. The entrance to eternal realms requires the death of one's body. People must go through the doorway called death in order to enter eternity. It is another realm and another dimension in which the physical laws and material properties of this world do not seem to apply. One must shed one's physical body. Only the soul of the person is left.

The second detail of this incident is that Lazarus' soul is carried away by angels. There is some form of transit function that the angels perform as the soul seemingly is incapable of traversing this distance or space on its own. There are implied elements that are not mentioned. Whatever had to take place for Lazarus to be evaluated and assigned to the place of the blessed dead is not mentioned. But that would also be a part of the transport of the angels. It is possible that there were different angels involved in the transport to the judgment and evaluation event and different angels that then transported Lazarus to the place of the blessed dead. Angels are seen throughout Scripture accomplishing and announcing things. They pop in and out of this material space-time dimensional universe. In this case they transport what is left of Lazarus after his body has quit functioning. Christians understand this as the soul and spirit. The soul/spirit is the essence of the person as well as the record and memories of who they are and all that they did and became. Clearly Jesus believes in and is testifying to life after death. The soul/spirit exists after death. It was not destroyed by death. It continues to exist. There is never the suggestion in this story that a soul can cease to exist.

The third detail of Jesus' story is that the poor man is carried to Abraham's bosom. This is the place of the blessed dead where people get comfort and help after their life (Luke 16:25). It is this detail of Abraham's bosom being in the same plane of existence as the place of the condemned that has caused many scholars to see a double compartment in Sheol -- one for the wicked dead and one for the blessed dead. The poor man Lazarus is carried away by the angels to the place of reward, comfort, and encouragement. Abraham's bosom is also called Paradise in this book (Luke 23:43).

The rich man's entrance into eternity is handled with much less detail and care. He is said to have died and then subsequently been buried. We are given only two specific details about the end of this man's life. He had an abundance of material goods, but he also died. He had to leave the material world through the doorway of death just like Lazarus did. He left his body behind and his soul/spirit traveled to eternal realms. We are not told in this passage that the angels came to carry him. But other passages of Scripture clearly tell us that angels are the transporters after death and/or are the instigators of death, even of the wicked (2 Samuel 24:16; 2 Kings 19:35; 1 Chronicles 21:15).

The rich man is buried as is Jewish tradition so that resurrection is possible. To bury someone speaks to the hope of resurrection as it speaks in Daniel 12:2.

Many of those who sleep in the dust of the ground will awake, these to everlasting life, but the others to disgrace and everlasting contempt.

WHAT DOES JESUS TELL US ABOUT THE SELF-INDULGENT RICH MAN IN THE AFTERLIFE?

There are five specific details in the next verse that Jesus mentions in regard to the rich man's situation in the afterlife.

First, the rich man finds himself in Hades or the place of the condemned dead. Hades is the Greek term for the place of the dead, both blessed and condemned. It is the holding tank before the final judgment at the end of history (Revelation 20:11-15). In the Old Testament the Hebrew word for this place is Sheol. It consisted of at least two compartments as Jesus describes here -- an upper compartment for the blessed dead and a lower compartment for the condemned dead. Most would understand this as upper and lower because the rich man lifts up his eyes to see Lazarus and Abraham. The architecture of hell will be dealt with in the next chapter. The rich man, just like Lazarus is, seemingly not able to move in or out of Hades without the angels. But he can desire to go to Abraham's bosom and those in Abraham's bosom can desire to go to Hades. There is the clear suggestion that people in both compartments of heaven can move around Hades or Sheol but that there are certain restrictions on their movement.

The second detail about the rich man's situation in the afterlife is that he is conscious. He is not unconscious. He has not ceased to exist. He has not been absorbed into some universal oneness. He is aware of his surroundings and knows where he is. This is not a foggy consciousness or some kind of limbo state. The rich man is aware of where he is and what is happening to him. He is in torment. Life does not end when we go through the doorway called death. We are still conscious after we die. I wish that I could talk with every person who is contemplating suicide as a way to end their troubles in this life. Remember that you are still conscious on the other side of the doorway called death and you have sealed your fate. Death does not end anything except your ability to choose and your animation of your earthly body.

A third detail which Jesus shares with us is that the rich man can lift up his eyes or look around him and be conscious of his surroundings and others. He has some kind of body or much of what is being talked about does not make sense. Many scholars believe that is a temporary body given to house the soul of the rich man and Lazarus as the final judgment has not taken place yet. The soul of the rich man has been put within a new body which can perceive, feel, hear, and interact with the realm of the dead all around it.

The fourth detail that Jesus gives us about the rich man's involvement in the eternal realms is that he is in torment. The word *torment* is the Greek word *basanos*, which means acute pain, torment, and difficulty. The word *being* in the NASB is the word *huparcho*, which carries with it the idea of being or being present in. It is the experience of the moment that the rich man is aware of. The Scriptures do not tell us what type of torment the rich man is experiencing. It is real and based upon other verses throughout Scripture (Romans 2:3-6; Psalm 62:12; Proverb 24:12; Matthew 16:27); it seems to grow out of the rich man's actions on the earth. The Scriptures seem to suggest that we store up treasure or wrath through our actions and choices in this life. There is nothing arbitrary or dictatorial about what happens to those in hell; it is their own stored actions and choices that are released upon them. Therefore whatever the torment is, it seems to be of their own making.

A fifth detail in this verse about the condition of the rich man in Hades is that he sees Abraham and the man who was at his front gate in the place of comfort and blessing a long ways from where he is. We can surmise that this means that there is some mental ability beyond what is present in this world in that he knows Abraham who he has never met, and he can perceive Lazarus and knows him as such. This means that he has a high level of mental clarity, can judge distances, and can make a judgment about Lazarus' seeming ability to come and help him. The speed at which he makes all of these judgments and the immediacy of his request suggests that he has done this kind of "help me" request before and is practiced at it.

Reflect on the details that Jesus supplies about the rich man. Jesus gives us enough about this wealthy individual to understand why this person was in hell.

WHAT IS THE ATTITUDE OF THE RICH MAN IN THE AFTERLIFE?

> **Luke 16:24** - *And he cried out and said, 'Father Abraham, have mercy on me, and send Lazarus so that he may dip the tip of his finger in water and cool off my tongue, for I am in agony in this flame.'*

We learn so much about the rich man through his interactions with Abraham in Hades that we can surmise what he must have been like when he was alive. He dies and wakes up in Hades on the wrong side of the chasm, and he is still superior in his attitude. He is immediately aware of inequity of the situation and superior position of poor man Lazarus. Even though he instinctively seems to know that he cannot get out of where he is, he believes that he needs a servant. His old ways of thinking have not been scrubbed from his mind but are even more striking. He still has the same "he is below me and I am above him" attitude controlling his reasoning. At least he doesn't have the gall to ask Abraham to come and serve him. Can't you just see this?

> "Abraham, I see you there not doing anything important except being in ease and comfort."

> "I need your help."

> "Yes, that's right, I need you to help me."

> "Don't you know who I am?"

There is a big part of me who would want to hear that exchange between Abraham and the rich man. I can also think of a lot of other exchanges that I would like to hear. But we are given this one and we need to glean all we can from this interchange between a pompous, self-focused, arrogant, rich man and Abraham in eternity.

The rich man feels safe in assuming that the same relative levels of social striations still exist. He is above the poor beggar even if he is in the condemned side of Hades. Therefore he can command him to do what is needed to make his stay more comfortable. The obvious point here is that the rich man has not changed his mind about how awful, proud, and bigoted he has been. He is worse. The selfishness that was in him when he was alive is still in him, corrupting and twisting him. It will continue to operate while he is in Hades. He will get more and more twisted.

One of the ideas that leaks through the pages of Scripture in this story and in other passages of Scripture is:

"WHAT YOU ARE IN THIS LIFE, YOU BECOME MORE OF IN THE AFTERLIFE"

If you are a little deceptive in this life, imagine what you will be like in 1,000 years as that grows and grows in the afterlife. The rich man was not different in the afterlife than he was in his earthly life. In fact he was more of what he was. He will continue to be a selfish, arrogant, and hedonistic person. And he will have thousands of years to allow what he is to fester and grow. If you are selfish, rebellious, and bigoted in this life, then you become more and more of that in the next life. Look at what **Romans 2:5-10** tells us about this idea:

> *But because of your stubbornness and unrepentant heart you are storing up wrath for yourself in the day of wrath and revelation of the righteous judgment of God, who*

What Does Jesus Tell Us About Hell?

> WILL RENDER TO EACH PERSON ACCORDING TO HIS DEEDS: *to those who by perseverance in doing good seek for glory and honor and immortality, eternal life; but to those who are selfishly ambitious and do not obey the truth, but obey unrighteousness, wrath and indignation. There will be tribulation and distress for every soul of man who does evil, of the Jew first and also of the Greek, but glory and honor and peace to everyone who does good, to the Jew first and also to the Greek.*

Let me hasten to add that the Scriptures are clear that only those who have been regenerated by the Holy Spirit can be pursuing the righteousness that God is talking about in this passage.

Look at **Revelation 22:11,14,15**. We see in this Scripture that the people who are in the lake of fire continue to practice the selfishness and sin that placed them there. They continue to be what they were -- continually churning out who they were and what they have become.

> *Let the one who does wrong, still do wrong; and the one who is filthy, still be filthy; and let the one who is righteous, still practice righteousness; and the one who is holy, still keep himself holy. Blessed are those who wash their robes, so that they may have the right to the tree of life, and may enter by the gates into the city. Outside are the dogs and the sorcerers and the immoral persons and the murderers and the idolaters, and everyone who loves and practices lying.*

Many have the idea that when people are assigned to Hades because of their sin, selfishness, rebellion, and growing wickedness, they will be repentant and plead for mercy. But this example from Jesus tells us the opposite. The people who would repent and plead for mercy did that before they got to this point and they were forgiven. Those who make it to the position of condemnation are unwilling to be separated from their choices, actions and attitudes. They did it their way and they are not going to accept any help -- even in the face of eternity.

Let's trace this thinking through the whole of the rich man's conversation with Abraham. He first wants Lazarus to be his servant. Second, he is unwilling to acknowledge the personhood and worth of Lazarus as God has valued him by placing him in Abraham's bosom. Third, he wants Lazarus to go warn his family and not anyone else. Everything about the dialogue of the rich man and Lazarus tells us that the rich man has not changed and has become even worse in that the corruption of selfishness does not allow him to focus on anyone except himself.

Some have objected to my harsh caricature of the rich man as selfish and completely absorbed in himself since he is very concerned that his family be warned about the realities of hell. This is not, however, an altruistic expression of selflessness within that culture. In that culture one did not exist as an individual but rather as a part of a family unit. An individual person was seen as a part of a family much the same way that a hand is seen as a part of someone's body. We do not know a hand separate from the body it is attached to. The singular unit was not the individual but the family. We are so individualistic presently that we see that any act of compassion that escapes our own preoccupied individual selves is seen as altruistic. They would have seen caring for your spouse, your children, and your parents as necessary and even selfish since any blessing your family received you received. They would have seen members of their family like their hand or their foot. One is not altruistic if your hand cares for your foot. One has not done a noble selfless act when your mind plans for your belly to be full. So for the rich man to care about whether his family would end up in hell is to be expected and is a part of his cultural, self-focused perspective. He does not express any concern for the rest of the town or the other beggars who were at his gate every day. He cared about himself and his own, period.

Another detail that resides in the midst of the dialogue between the rich man and Abraham is that he is demanding. He is not making a request as a penitent person but instead as a person who has every right to demand what he wants. Yes, he is superior in his attitude but he is also demanding. It is possible to be superior without being demanding, but the rich man is both. I want what I want when I want it. This is the motto of every two-year old, and it is the creed of every person in the flames of Hades. Without the grace of God to soften his self-centeredness, it continues to grow and become demanding with the father of his religious heritage, Abraham.

As the dialogue with Abraham goes on, he displays not only his continuing feeling of superiority and a demanding tone but finally an argumentative posture. He disagrees with Abraham even though he knows who he is. It is helpful to see that this "I am right and I know more than you" is still in a person as they move into eternity. It has not been flushed out by the basic judgment that took place to put them in the condemned side of Hades. In fact, this argumentativeness seems to be confirmed by the process of death. Many believe that death strips us of all our bad parts and leaves only the good. But this is only true of those who have surrendered to Christ and have allowed their faith in Christ to let him perform whatever surgery He needs to make them fit for heaven. This also tells us that God is under no requirement to straighten out people's erroneous views about the world, the afterlife, God, and their life on earth. People are allowed to reject God and Christ and never really grasp the truth of life.

God allowed the rich man to continue in his argumentative state, his demanding nature, and his superior attitude.

What do we learn about hell from Abraham's response back to the rich man?

Luke 16:25,26 - But Abraham said, "Child, remember that during your life you received your good things, and likewise Lazarus bad things; but now he is being comforted here, and you are in agony."

And besides all this, between us and you there is a great chasm fixed, so that those who wish to come over from here to you will not be able, and that none may cross over from there to us.

1. Abraham expects the rich man to remember his life and his recent preliminary evaluation which preceded his assignment into the condemned sections of Sheol.

In order to understand Abraham's response to the rich man, we must understand what has to have taken place before this exchange. One cannot be assigned to the place of the blessed or the place of the damned without a review of one's life. A judgment is required (Hebrews 9:27). Therefore it is not possible that the rich man is arbitrarily assigned to flames and the poor man is randomly assigned to the place of comfort. In fact, Abraham alludes to this review and its obvious consequences when he answers the rich man's question.

Abraham is asking the rich man to recall the review of his life that the angels and God the judge conducted. Abraham recalls this review and how the rich man had chosen to live selfishly and with a complete focus on getting good things for himself and with no thought of being a distribution point for good things. God clearly gave the rich man the ability to collect good things and instead of being a river of blessings to many, the rich man became a reservoir, hoarding the resources to himself. He dammed up the resources that should have flowed through him to others and spent them completely on himself. It was this greed and self-seeking which damned him to the wrong side of the chasm. Abraham essentially says, "Remember the evaluation of your life and your squandering of the good things God gave you and how your selfishness inflicted radical hardship on Lazarus who was prepared to help people."

Remember, therefore, when you read this question of the rich man that he has already been through his review and preliminary judgment which did not go well. He knows that he is assigned to hell because he lived a life of wanton disregard for those who were in need around him. The prime example of his selfishness and sinfulness is the poor man Lazarus, who he is still trying to control, abuse, and project his superiority over which was most likely pointed out in his just concluded judgment. Abraham reminds him of all these things with just one phrase: *You received your good things (which you refused to pass along to others in need) and he received bad things (because you did not share with him even though he was at your front gate).* The rich man did not live according to the greatest commandments given to us in **Matthew 22:37-40:**

> *And He said to him,* "YOU SHALL LOVE THE LORD YOUR GOD WITH ALL YOUR HEART, AND WITH ALL YOUR SOUL, AND WITH ALL YOUR MIND. *This is the great and foremost commandment. The second is like it,* YOU SHALL LOVE YOUR NEIGHBOR AS YOURSELF. *On these two commandments depend the whole Law and the Prophets.*"

The rich man did not have faith in God to multiply the benefits that he had been given if he was generous to those clearly in need. Throughout the rich man's life he had ignored the righteous opportunities that came across his path to pursue his own pleasure. He was out for what he could have, experience, and control and it was now costing him.

It is important to mention the righteousness which comes through faith as no one is capable of accomplishing the righteousness that comes through works. It was through faith that Abraham was considered righteous because he believed God and it was reckoned to him as righteousness (Romans 4:1-5). David is also cited in Romans as one who was counted as righteous because of his faith not his works (Romans 4:6-10). Jesus himself says that the righteousness that people must have to be declared fit for the kingdom of God is accomplished through faith and not through works (John 3:16; 6:29).

It is also clear that the faith that saves produces works that glorify God and show faith's existence (James 2:14-26). God is looking for the faith when the review is done, but He is also looking for the evidence of the faith. It is this lack of evidence of true faith that the rich man lacks. All of the evidence of his life says that he lived for himself and never expressed true faith in God and went outside his own selfish pursuits (Romans 2:5-11).

2. HELL IS A PLACE OF JUSTICE AND EQUITY.

One of the clear ideas about eternity is that it is a place of justice. Even if justice is missed or delayed in our earthly existence, it will not be in eternity. All the evidence will be brought out. Even your own thoughts, secret conversations, and hidden actions will be made known (Matthew 10:26; 12:36,37; Luke 8:17; 1 Corinthians 3:12-15).

It is this fundamental element of justice that Abraham is alluding to in his response to the rich man. He is saying that you got more than your share of good things when you were alive; don't forget that, buddy. In fact, the reason why you got more than your share of good things is because you refused to pass them on to those around you in need.

The oppression and greed of the rich man begins to be recompensed in this place called Hades or hell. He clearly oppressed the poor man and he clearly lived a selfish, indulgent life when some of those resources that he was spending on himself clearly should have been passed on to those around him. Justice will be done to those who are perpetrators of oppression, violence, affliction, and the like. Abraham reminds the rich man about his review. You received all the good you are going to receive because of how you jealously clung to every good thing that came to you and only passed on bad things to people like the poor man, Lazarus. God will judge people according to their deeds. Hell is the place where the truth of **Romans 2:5,6** begins to be brought to fruition:

> *But because of your stubbornness and unrepentant heart you are storing up wrath for yourself in the day of wrath and revelation of the righteous judgment of God, who* WILL RENDER TO EACH PERSON ACCORDING TO HIS DEEDS.

The rich man believed that what came across his life was his to use as he saw fit, but this is not the truth. We are often given blessings that are not for us but are for someone downstream. We are to let this blessing flow through to them. We are the middleman who is to convey the goods to them.

This issue of justice, fairness, and equity is huge to us. We all have an innate sense of when something is not right or fair. Almost all of us are aware of people who have gotten away with some crime, wound, swindle, or heinous action in their earthly life. They did not pay the price that they should have paid. Hell is the place where they will pay unless they repent while on earth and allow Christ to pay instead. One of the great truths of the gospel is that we can offer to people true forgiveness for their sins through the death of Christ. Justice will be done to the individual or to Christ. But justice will be done.

3. Abraham is gracious in his answer rather than blunt.

It is amazing isn't it that the rich man can act like he has the right to command Abraham to do this and do that and yet Abraham does not react. Abraham, instead, reminds the rich man that his life has been reviewed and he made a selfish mess of it. This suggests that the review which Abraham has been through has transformed him, leaving only the good parts to be left to grow and develop. Abraham has had the gracious parts of his personality brought out to great degree. Won't that be great to not react as we normally would in our flesh to the stupid questions of others but instead to treat people with dignity and respect.

I know of a number of people who are scared to death that if they do go to heaven that they will mess it up and be kicked out because of some angry, unkind, selfish, or offensive thing that they will do. But the good news is that that won't happen. The Apostle John tells us that when we see Him, we will be like Him (1 John 3:1-3). We will be transformed into the likeness of His glory. We will not have those parts of our personality left in us; so we will respond to others with kindness, love, grace, and joy just like Abraham did to the rich man. We will actually act out the fruit of the spirit. Think about living in a place where everyone is consistently living out the fruit of the spirit for each other. Now I don't believe that we will be pushovers with no backbone or radically naïve. We will be wise, loving, and strong. Remember, Abraham was not a pushover in this case, but he was not needlessly rude and arrogant.

4. THERE ARE LIMITS AND BOUNDARIES IN ETERNITY AND IN HELL.

Abraham explains to the rich man the rules of this eternal place. No one can trade places no matter how much they may want to. It is not allowed. What is amazing about Abraham's explanation is that it is clear in the way he tells the rules that those in Abraham's bosom would want to go to Hades and those in hell would want to come to Abraham's bosom. God instituted rules so that couldn't happen. The people who are in "heaven" are of a nature and orientation that they want to help and serve so much so that they would respond to the pleas to come down to hell. It just proves that they belong in "heaven" that much more. Those in hell want to cheat, steal, lie, and deceive themselves out of the consequences of their life on earth and yet they are prevented. They did not accept the consequences of their lives on earth, and they are not about to start now.

5. THE RICH MAN IS SURPRISINGLY UNINTERESTED IN WHAT IS SUPREMELY IMPORTANT TO US. HOW LONG WILL THIS LAST? WHY AM I HERE?

Those in hell are not interested in what we would want to know. This is not a philosophical game to them. They are in a real place with real agony. They have been brought to this place by their own choices, actions, and words. They have built the house that they are now living in. This is a hard truth with real motivation to warn people about a life of wanton selfishness. Those in hell seem to know that they are in the wrong place, and it won't help to know the how or the why. Or they already know the how and the why. As I have mentioned, I believe that since God is not arbitrary there is a preliminary judgment that the rich man has been through, and then he was placed into the torment of hell where his own deeds stored up wrath and agony that will be released upon him (Romans 2:5-10).

The rich man avoids a lot of the questions that we would think he would want to ask. Why am I here? How long will this last? What do I have to do to get out? He asks none of these questions because the previous review of his life answers those questions. All he is concerned about is easing the pain that his past choices in life have brought upon him.

Chapter 2

The Architecture of Hell

"Hell is the great compliment to the reality of human freedom and the dignity of human choice."[1]

Let's ask ourselves some more questions regarding Jesus' testimony about hell and the place of the dead. We must remember that Jesus is describing the place of the dead before any of the cataclysmic events surrounding his death, burial, and resurrection. He was crucified, was buried, descended to Sheol, rose from the dead, and then ascended to the Father.

As the diagrams in this chapter will show, Sheol is the Hebrew word for the place of the dead -- both the righteous dead and the unrighteous dead. The word Sheol has also been used to refer specifically to just the lower compartment of the dead. This, at times, leads to confusion regarding what is the precise definition of the Hebrew word Sheol. Another confusing fact is that the upper compartment of Sheol, which in Jesus' description is the place of the righteous dead (Abraham and Lazarus), is not heaven but is a place of waiting until the righteous dead get to go to heaven. This seems to be where Samuel comes from in 1 Samuel 28:13-19 and where Moses and Elijah come from in Matthew 17.

Now let's remind ourselves again of Jesus' description in **Luke 16:19-29**:

> *Now there was a rich man, and he habitually dressed in purple and fine linen, joyously living in splendor every day. And a poor man named Lazarus was laid at his gate, covered with sores, and longing to be fed with the crumbs which were falling from the rich man's table; besides, even the dogs were coming and licking his sores. Now the poor man died and was carried away by the angels to Abraham's bosom; and the rich man also died and was buried. In Hades he lifted up his eyes, being in torment, and saw Abraham far away and Lazarus in his bosom. And he cried out and said, "Father Abraham, have mercy on me, and send Lazarus so that he may dip the tip of his finger in water and cool off my tongue, for I am in agony in this flame." But Abraham said, "Child, remember that during your life you received your good things, and likewise Lazarus bad things; but now he is being comforted here, and you are in agony. And besides all this, between us and you there is a great chasm fixed, so that those who wish to come over from here to you will not be able, and that none may cross over from there to us." And he said, "Then I beg you, father, that you send him to my father's house -- for I have five brothers -- in order that he may warn them, so that they will not also come to this place of torment." But Abraham said, "They have Moses and the Prophets; let them hear them." But he said, "No, father Abraham, but if someone goes to them from the dead, they will repent!" But he said to him, "If they do not listen to Moses and the Prophets, they will not be persuaded even if someone rises from the dead."*

WHAT IS THE STATE OF THOSE IN HELL?

Let's restate the information that Jesus is giving us about hell in a very direct form. We learn the following facts: there are two compartments, people in hell have had a review of their life, there are flames, there is consciousness, there is real existence, there is memory, there is torment, there is agony, there are limits and rules, and there is awareness of others.

There are at least two compartments. An upper compartment called Abraham's bosom, paradise, or the home of the blessed dead and a lower compartment, called Hades or hell. There is a great chasm between the two compartments that is large enough to not allow the blessed side to come to the aid of the tormented side, nor the tormented side to come to the blessed side. There is communication from both of the compartments to each other. There also seems to be communication and interaction within the upper compartment. There is some suggestion from the passage in Luke 16 and some in Jude that there is a high level of isolation in the lower compartment.

> **Jude 1:6,12,13** - *And angels who did not keep their own domain, but abandoned their proper abode, He has kept in eternal bonds under darkness for the judgment of the great day. These are the men who are hidden reefs in your love feasts when they feast with you without fear, caring for themselves; clouds without water, carried along by winds; autumn trees without fruit, doubly dead, uprooted; wild waves of the sea, casting up their own shame like foam; wandering stars, for whom the black darkness has been reserved forever.*

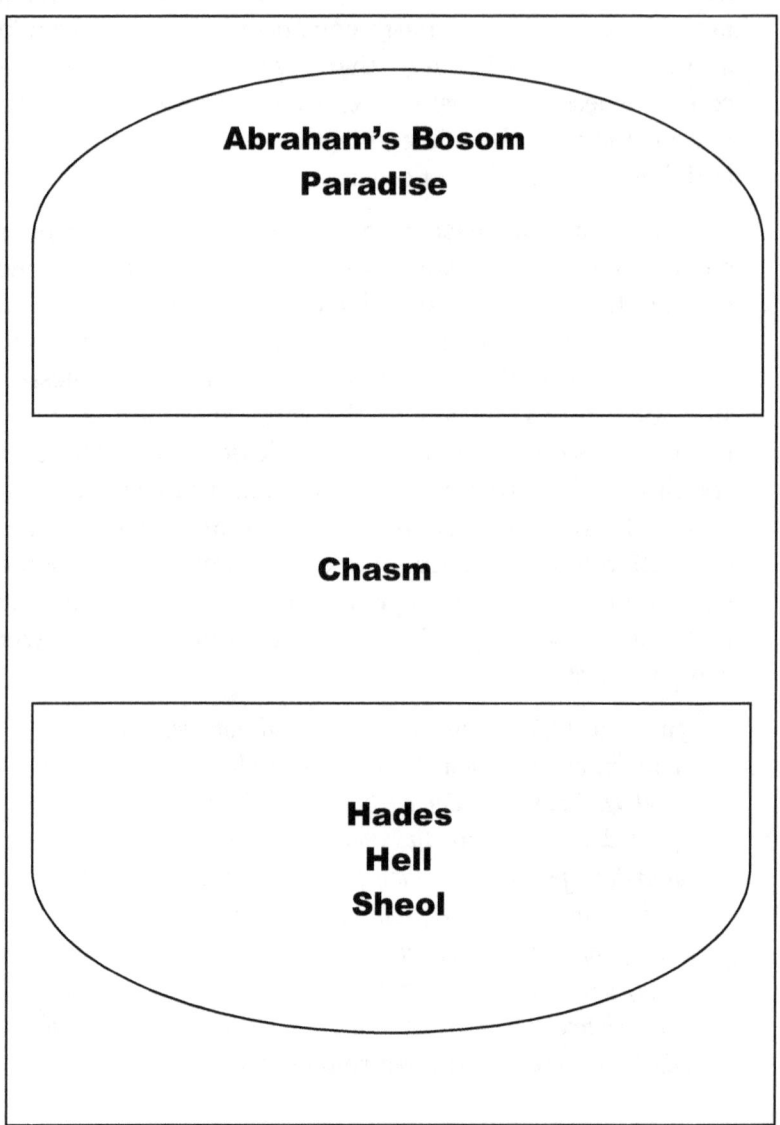

The Architecture of Hell

This is the way that Jesus relates the state of the blessed and the damned in the afterlife in Sheol. Sheol is that plane of existence that contains both the blessed and the damned prior to the death, burial, and resurrection of Christ.

There is a suggestion in other parts of Scripture that there is a sub-compartment of the condemned dead which is called the bottomless pit, the abyss, or Tartarus in the Greek -- in which certain angelic spirits who rebelled from God's boundaries are kept until the final judgment. Notice the following verses:

Luke 8:31 - *They were imploring Him (Jesus) not to command them to go away into the abyss.*

2 Peter 2:4 - *For if God did not spare angels when they sinned, but cast them into hell and committed them to pits of darkness, reserved for judgment.*

Revelation 9:1,2 - *Then the fifth angel sounded, and I saw a star from heaven which had fallen to the earth; and the key of the bottomless pit was given to him. He opened the bottomless pit, and smoke went up out of the pit, like the smoke of a great furnace; and the sun and the air were darkened by the smoke of the pit.*

Revelation 20:1-3 - *Then I saw an angel coming down from heaven, holding the key of the abyss and a great chain in his hand. And he laid hold of the dragon, the serpent of old, who is the devil and Satan, and bound him for a thousand years; and he threw him into the abyss, and shut it and sealed it over him, so that he would not deceive the nations any longer, until the thousand years were completed; after these things he must be released for a short time.*

SHEOL

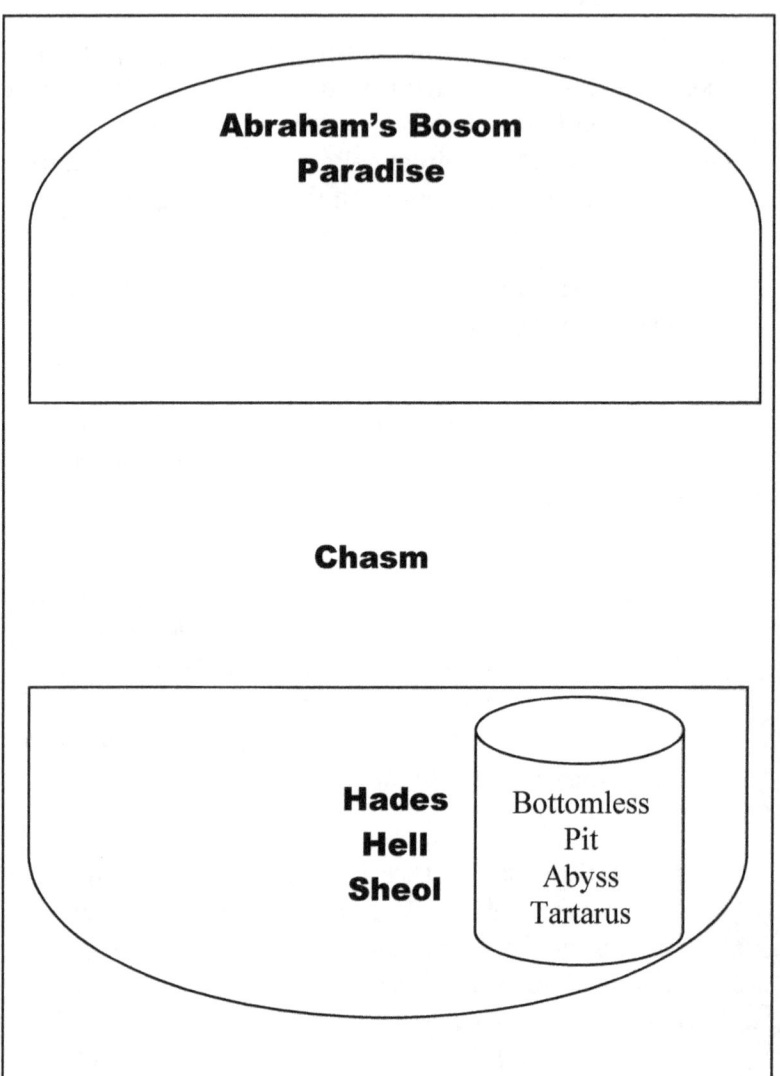

Many scholars believe that when Jesus died and subsequently rose again, He emptied this upper compartment by taking those in it with Him to enjoy the heavenly realms.

> **Ephesians 4:8-10** - *Therefore it says, "WHEN HE ASCENDED ON HIGH, HE LED CAPTIVE A HOST OF CAPTIVES, AND HE GAVE GIFTS TO MEN." (Now this expression, "He ascended," what does it mean except that He also had descended into the lower parts of the earth? He who descended is Himself also He who ascended far above all the heavens, so that He might fill all things.)*

This would agree with 1 Peter 3:17-20 and Jesus' announcement to those spirits who are now in prison. Either He announced that He was taking those in the upper compartment, or He announced that those in the lower compartment had lost because of His sacrifice for the sins of the world.

> **1 Peter 3:17-20** - *For it is better, if God should will it so, that you suffer for doing what is right rather than for doing what is wrong. For Christ also died for sins once for all, the just for the unjust, so that He might bring us to God, having been put to death in the flesh, but made alive in the spirit; in which also He went and made proclamation to the spirits now in prison, who once were disobedient, when the patience of God kept waiting in the days of Noah, during the construction of the ark, in which a few, that is, eight persons, were brought safely through the water.*

There has been some kind of judgment or preliminary review of life which places the person in the category they are assigned (Hebrews 9:27). God is not arbitrary and he does not assign people randomly to blessing or damnation. He has reasons. He spells out those qualifying reasons throughout Scripture: the righteousness which comes through faith (Romans 4:1-10; John 3:16; John 6:29).

THERE IS FLAME.

It is clearly a different kind of flame than the type of flame we understand currently. People who are in the midst of flames in our universe do not carry on conversations. They do not argue. They are not superior in their attitude. They do not notice people and situations a long ways away. So whatever this flame is, it is not the same kind of flame we are used to. Flame seems to be the most apropos description that Jesus and the rich man can use to describe what he is in that we in our world would understand. Flame is the way that those in hell describe what is happening to them, and it is the way that Jesus chooses to describe it. Flame in our world is a consumptive process. So it may be better to understand that the person is being consumed in some other way than the way we think of flame working in this world.

The flame here in eternity seems more like the burning bush episode in **Exodus 3:1-5**:

> *Now Moses was pasturing the flock of Jethro his father-in-law, the priest of Midian; and he led the flock to the west side of the wilderness and came to Horeb, the mountain of God. The angel of the LORD appeared to him in a blazing fire from the midst of a bush; and he looked, and behold, the bush was burning with fire, yet the bush was not consumed. So Moses said, "I must turn aside now and see this marvelous sight, why the bush is not burned up." When the LORD saw that he turned aside to look, God called to him from the midst of the bush and said, "Moses, Moses!" And he said, "Here I am." Then He said, "Do not come near here; remove your sandals*

from your feet, for the place on which you are standing is holy ground."

There is true flame or what looks like flame but the bush is not consumed. It would seem that in hell there is flame but the person is not consumed. What the flame does, how is it like flame, and what is its fuel are all questions that at this point cannot be answered. But clearly eternal flame is not like earthly flame in some very important ways. Much of the imagery, horrors, distortions, and illogical conclusions regarding hell have been about the flames. They are not flames from this world or there would be no talking, no planning, no problem solving, no arguing, and no continuous burning without consumption.

We have a number of Scriptures that refer to flames in the eternal state or that come from God and these seem to refer to the evaluation of God or the presence of God in evaluation (1 Corinthians 3:11-13; Revelation 1:12-15). It is entirely possible that the flames are the actual presence of God in holiness and righteousness constantly evaluating the actions, thoughts, and motives of those who have rejected God's offer of forgiveness.

One of the truths of the future of the damned is that they will be in the midst of flames. Some have understood that those in hell will be separated from God. This is not technically true. The damned will be separated from the grace and mercy of God. They, however, will know the unrelenting presence of God in righteousness, holiness, and wrath. Some have suggested that the flames of the burning bush -- which is a manifestation of the presence of God -- will be heaven from those who are fit for it and hell for those who have demanded their own independent way.

THERE IS CONSCIOUSNESS.

Life is not over after the body ceases to function. The rich man, as well as Lazarus, is aware of their circumstances and reactive to them. The rich man has perception of distant as well as immediate objects. He is able to do problem solving and argumentation. Therefore this is not a zombie life without reasoning and interaction. Abraham's conversation tells us that on both sides of the eternal divide there is consciousness and interaction.

Materialistic philosophy believes that the brain is the seat of consciousness and that we are nothing more than a computer made of meat, which springs to life some form of collective consciousness because of the millions of neurons firing. This is not true. The brain, at best, houses or stores some form of our consciousness. The Scriptures are quite clear in this passage and in others that our consciousness survives the death of our bodies. Our consciousness resides in our soul, which is immaterial.

There have been a number of fascinating experiments done on people during brain surgery when the patients must be conscious while their brains are exposed. Certain areas of the brain are stimulated and the patients' arm moves. The doctors have asked the patients why they made their arm move. The patients respond that they did not move their arm but that the doctors made their arm move. The patients were aware that it was not them who made their arm move even though the stimulation to move the arm came through the same neural pathway as their consciousness uses. Consciousness resides apart from the brain and survives brain death. (*The Spiritual Brain: A Neuroscientists evidence for the existence of the soul* by Mario Beauregard and Denyse O'Leary. *Immortality, the Other Side of Death,* by Gary R. Habermas and J.P. Moreland).

The Architecture of Hell

THERE IS SOME TYPE OF REAL EXISTENCE.

The consciousness is in some form. The rich man is able to feel, perceive, understand and problem-solve. These things require some type of existence anchored in some time and/or spatial dimensionality. It could be in a pure soul/spirit form that we are unfamiliar with or it could be in some temporary physical form that allows it to have sensation, communication, limited mobility, and location. Some have argued for a temporary physical form to house the soul before judgment day and a final physical form. For how can a pure spirit/soul feel pain as the rich man is feeling in this situation? But the rebuttal to that argument is that the Devil and his angels who are pure spirit are cast into the lake of fire (Revelation 20:10) and whatever the lake of fire is, it is both a containment vessel and a place of justice for them. They are held captive there by the boundaries of the lake of fire and the flames of that place. They are pure spirit beings and they are tormented by the flames. They do not have a body to destroy. They are consumed -- but not completely --by some type of burning. It would seem to be their own actions, choices, and attitudes are the flames that they exist within.

> **Romans 2:2-6** - *And we know that the judgment of God rightly falls upon those who practice such things. But do you suppose this, O man, when you pass judgment on those who practice such things and do the same yourself, that you will escape the judgment of God? Or do you think lightly of the riches of His kindness and tolerance and patience, not knowing that the kindness of God leads you to repentance? But because of your stubbornness and unrepentant heart you are storing up wrath for yourself in the day of wrath and revelation of the righteous judgment of God, who WILL RENDER TO EACH PERSON ACCORDING TO HIS DEEDS*

Why There Has To Be A Hell

THERE IS MEMORY.

The rich man can remember who he is and what station he had in life. The rich man can see and recognize people like Lazarus who he knew in life. He also seems to have a heightened sense of awareness in that he can recognize people who he has never met; i.e., Father Abraham. This is important to note because it means that all of our memories are not expunged at the point of death. This suggests why God is said to dry every tear and comfort those in heaven (Revelation 21:4). Those in heaven do remember what took place on earth but they need to have their memories reframed and redeemed.

THERE IS TORMENT.

The rich man is in torment and he calls what he is experiencing agony. What is fascinating is that he carries on a conversation in the midst of the torment and agony. As I have stated previously, this is not the same type of agony and torment that we would normally associate with flames in our world. In our world if a person were truly on fire, all this conversation and noticing people would not be taking place. There is some form of constant pain and difficulty that the rich man is aware of and wants to alleviate. He feels as though just some cold water will alleviate his agony to some degree. Abraham does not tell him that it won't work or that it is not that kind of physical pain; he just tells him that his underlying, selfish superiority will not be satisfied.

Some have suggested that the story that Jesus uses to talk about torturers in a debtors' prison will be what the demons do to the wicked in the afterlife (Matthew 18:34). There is no suggestion in the story or anywhere else in Scripture that the physical jailers in the debtors' prisons of the first century are analogous to the work of demons in the afterlife.

Instead of that erroneous view, notice in the following passages that each time torment is mentioned, it is about evil being in the presence of God or righteous people being in the presence of evil.

> **Matthew 8:29** - *And they cried out, saying, "What business do we have with each other, Son of God? Have You come here to torment us before the time?"*

> **2 Corinthians 12:7** - *Because of the surpassing greatness of the revelations, for this reason, to keep me from exalting myself, there was given me a thorn in the flesh, a messenger of Satan to torment me—to keep me from exalting myself!*

> **2 Peter 2:8** - *(for by what he saw and heard that righteous man, while living among them, felt his righteous soul tormented day after day by their lawless deeds)*

> **Revelation 11:10** - *And those who dwell on the earth will rejoice over them and celebrate; and they will send gifts to one another, because these two prophets tormented those who dwell on the earth.*

> **Revelation 14:10** - *he also will drink of the wine of the wrath of God, which is mixed in full strength in the cup of His anger; and he will be tormented with fire and brimstone in the presence of the holy angels and in the presence of the Lamb.*

Revelation 14:11 - *And the smoke of their* <u>torment</u> *goes up forever and ever; they have no rest day and night, those who worship the beast and his image, and whoever receives the mark of his name.*

Revelation 18:7 - *To the degree that she glorified herself and lived sensuously, to the same degree give* <u>her torment and mourning</u>; *for she says in her heart, 'I sit as a queen and I am not a widow, and will never see mourning.'*

Revelation 20:10 - *And the devil who deceived them was thrown into the lake of fire and brimstone, where the beast and the false prophet are also; and* <u>they will be tormented day and night</u> *forever and ever.*

The torment of the damned may be the growing sinfulness, selfishness, and wickedness in themselves constantly being exposed to the righteousness and holiness of God. Imagine what it would be like to be committed to selfishness and rebellion and to be constantly surrounded by the person and presence from whom you want to rebel. It would be torment.

THERE ARE LIMITS.

Abraham makes it clear to the rich man as well as to Lazarus that there is no way for the divide to be crossed. This is very interesting in that it suggests boundaries exist within hell. It also suggests that those in Abraham's bosom would cross over to aid those in hell if they could and those in hell would cross over and steal the blessings of Abraham's bosom if they could. This is not allowed. People stay true to their nature. God has put limits so that the blessed cannot be conned by the damned. He puts boundaries on the damned so that they can no longer oppress and afflict the blessed. Heaven is a place of openness and transparency. We do not need to cover ourselves because no one will be in heaven who will nurse their selfishness to harm other's.

We can speculate why the limits on those in heaven and those in hell exist, but we are not told. These limits suggest that there are elements and conditions of the afterlife that we do not understand and that could be perverted if the proper controls were not put into place. Some type of quarantine exists around hell and the rules surrounding movement in and out are very specific.

What is the state of those in Abraham's bosom?

What does Jesus tell us about the place called Abraham's bosom or paradise? It is a place of comfort, interaction, limits, perception of others, desire to help and serve, and some form of mobility.

There is comfort.

The idea of comfort and care is a primary theme of heaven. It is not a place of strutting and celebrating because you are there. There seems to be the understanding that you don't belong there and you have profound sense of humility. There is some form of remediation taking place for the difficulties and inequities of life on earth.

There are others interacting with the person. The rich man can see that Lazarus is being attended to and comforted by others. We are not told if it is angels or other individuals, but it is some form of personal interaction that is not happening in the place where the rich man resides. It is this interaction with others and this personal contact that is most blessed about Abraham's bosom. Jude reminds us that those who are rebellious, sensual, and selfish are like wandering stars headed to the black darkness.

> **Jude 1:12-13** - *These are the men who are hidden reefs in your love feasts when they feast with you without fear, caring for themselves; clouds without water, carried along by winds; autumn trees without fruit, doubly dead, uprooted; wild waves of the sea, casting up their own shame like foam; wandering stars, for whom the black darkness has been reserved forever.*

It is the alienation from others and the aloneness with the choices that we have made that will constitute the pain of hell. We will be living in the house we have built of our own decisions and actions. Therefore it is the gracious gift of others, both old and new, that will be the delight of heaven. Alienation is one of the chief consequences of sin, rebellion, and selfishness. It isolates even while it promises friends and intimacy.

THERE ARE LIMITS.

This is shocking to many of us. But there are limits in Abraham's bosom. There are some things that the people of heaven would like to do that they are not allowed to do. Abraham says that there is a chasm that is fixed between Abraham's bosom and Hades so that those who would want to go from the heavenly side to the hellish side to render the aid that the rich man is asking for would not be able to do so. Isn't that fascinating? The servant's heart of the people in the place of blessing would prompt them to care and want to alleviate the suffering of those in hell. But they are not allowed. We are told of a few other limits (the need for angelic transport to enter and the inability to get a message out), and we can assume there may be others.

Just as there needs to be limits on love and giving in this life (Philemon 1:6-8), so there is a need for limits and discernment on love, giving, and serving in the next life. Radical-giving love is not always the best answer for the person or the community as a whole. It is always the place to start, but one must be willing to realize that this impulse at certain places can be damaging and destructive.

THERE IS PERCEPTION OF OTHERS.

Abraham is aware of others -- both in the good side of Sheol and the bad side of Sheol. He knows who they are and what they need. This observation is crucial because some have thought that the place of the dead is a foggy land where no perceptions of the past, people, or the future are possible but this does not seem to be the case. Jesus helps us with this reality further on the Mount of Transfiguration when Moses and Elijah appear and begin discussing Christ's life, death, and resurrection. The two great pillars of the faith, Moses and Elijah, are aware of each other and are interested in conversing with Christ (Matthew 17:3-6). Abraham is much more aware of the people around him and his surroundings than those in the place of the condemned.

THERE IS DESIRE TO HELP AND TO SERVE.

This idea that the people in the afterlife still want to serve, help, and give would be a further suggestion that what you became in this life is what you will continue to grow in during the next life. Those who are in the blessed place in the afterlife are those who lived out of faith by loving God and loving others. This became their automatic response. This desire to love and serve was them, and it continues into eternity.

The fascinating book, *Shantung Compound*, by Sheldon Gilkey shows this truth of what you were before a crisis is what you will display no matter what your circumstances. "Shantung Compound" is the true story of those who were imprisoned in a Japanese prisoner-of-war camp in mainland China during World War II. Everyone there lost everything and had to remake themselves in the compound through their service to one another. All measure of status and privilege were stripped away. There were those who were a credit to the name of Christ through their unfailing service in the camp and there were those who did little or no work as was their custom before their incarceration. Gilkey spends considerable time describing missionaries and pastors who were useless when it came to real work. Gilkey includes the gripping story of Eric Liddell, the Olympic champion of *Chariots of Fire* fame, serving with joy and tireless devotion. He gave of himself like people would expect a Christian would. He died well respected and loved by those who observed him every day in the camps, while those with no credentials demanded to be served even though they contributed nothing to the survival of the camp.

THERE IS THE ABILITY TO MOVE.

Abraham's declaration of limits on the movement for those in the place of the blessed and likewise restrictions on the movement of those in the place of the damned would suggest that people in both places can move and explore. They are not allowed to go to the other compartment, but they are mobile. Remember that they needed the angels to get to these places initially. But now they are able to explore within their respective compartments but not cross over to the other compartment.

There is so much insight and truth in what Jesus tells us, and it should motivate us to share the good news with those we know so that they will escape the destruction that is coming. It is a sad thing that our understanding of hell has become so distant because it no longer serves as a motivator for us to share with others the wonderful news that we do not have to end up in the place called hell. God can be our portion and our righteousness. He offers us love, and we must make sure that we do not slap his hand away.

CHAPTER 3

THE FUTURE OF HELL

"At some point in the 1960's hell disappeared. No one could say for certain when this happened. First, it was there and then it wasn't. Different people became aware of the disappearance of hell at different times."[1]

As a culture, those in America and Europe have largely stopped thinking or planning about hell. They have moved past any negative afterlife as a possibility. Because of western civilization's almost complete embrace of undirected, mechanistic evolution there is no room for an afterlife, let alone a negative one. The obvious inadequacy and bankruptcy of the materialistic worldview is forcing people to grapple with the spirit world, the afterlife, judgment day, and to reexamine the truth about hell. It is time to get a more accurate understanding of hell and its future. Many people mistakenly believe that hell will go on forever. It will not!!!

The good news is that God will do away with hell in the future. The bad news is that God transfers all the people that were in hell to the lake of fire. Look at the Scripture:

Revelation 20:11-15 - *Then I saw a great white throne and Him who sat upon it, from whose presence earth and heaven fled away, and no place was found for them. And I saw the dead, the great and the small, standing before the throne, and books were opened; and another book was opened, which is the book of life; and the dead were judged from the things which were written in the books, according to their deeds. And the sea gave up the dead which were in it, and death and Hades gave up the dead which were in them; and they were judged, every one of them according to their deeds. Then death and Hades were thrown into the lake of fire. This is the second death, the lake of fire. And if anyone's name was not found written in the book of life, he was thrown into the lake of fire.*

It seems best to try and understand hell through dividing its existence into three distinct phases: the past, the present, and the future. Examine the diagrams on the next few pages.

The past: Where hell was one of two different parts of the larger realm of the dead, Sheol. Hell is the lower compartment (Luke 16:16-29).

SHEOL

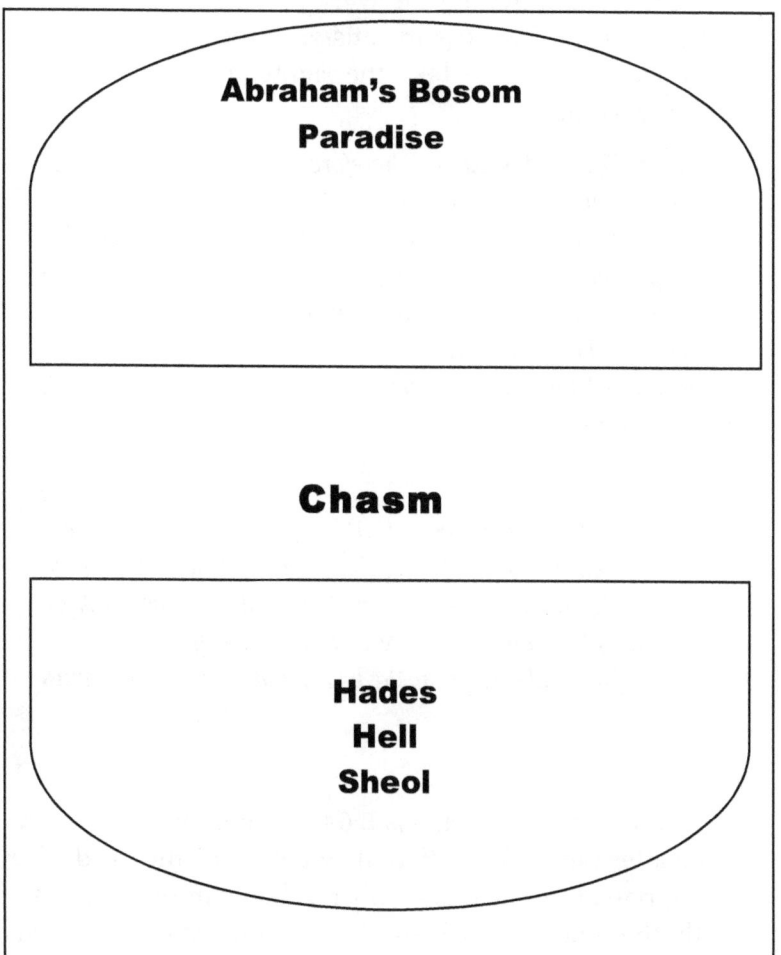

The present: The present condition of hell is where hell is only the holding tank for the unrighteous dead as they wait for judgment day. The upper compartment has been completely emptied by the work of Christ. The work that Christ did on the cross in satisfying the payment for our sins allowed Him to take the righteous dead out of the upper chamber.

> **Ephesians 4:8-10** - *Therefore it says, "WHEN HE ASCENDED ON HIGH, HE LED CAPTIVE A HOST OF CAPTIVES, AND HE GAVE GIFTS TO MEN." (Now this expression, "He ascended," what does it mean except that He also had descended into the lower parts of the earth? He who descended is Himself also He who ascended far above all the heavens, so that He might fill all things.)*

> **2 Corinthians 5:6-8** - (KJV 1900) *Therefore we are always confident, knowing that, whilst we are at home in the body, we are absent from the Lord: For we walk by faith, not by sight: We are confident, I say, and willing rather to be absent from the body, and to be present with the Lord.*

Notice in 2 Corinthians 5:6-8 there is no intermediate state after people die before they get to see the Lord. They are in one of two places -- either at home in their bodies or with the Lord in heaven. This is different than Jesus' description of Sheol in Luke 16. Heaven is now the place where people go who die in the Lord. They do not go to Sheol and have to wait for the death of Christ to set them free.

The Future of Hell

The upper compartment of Sheol has been emptied at Christ's death, resurrection, and ascension. Those who were waiting for Christ's ultimate sacrifice for them have been released to enjoy the direct presence of God.

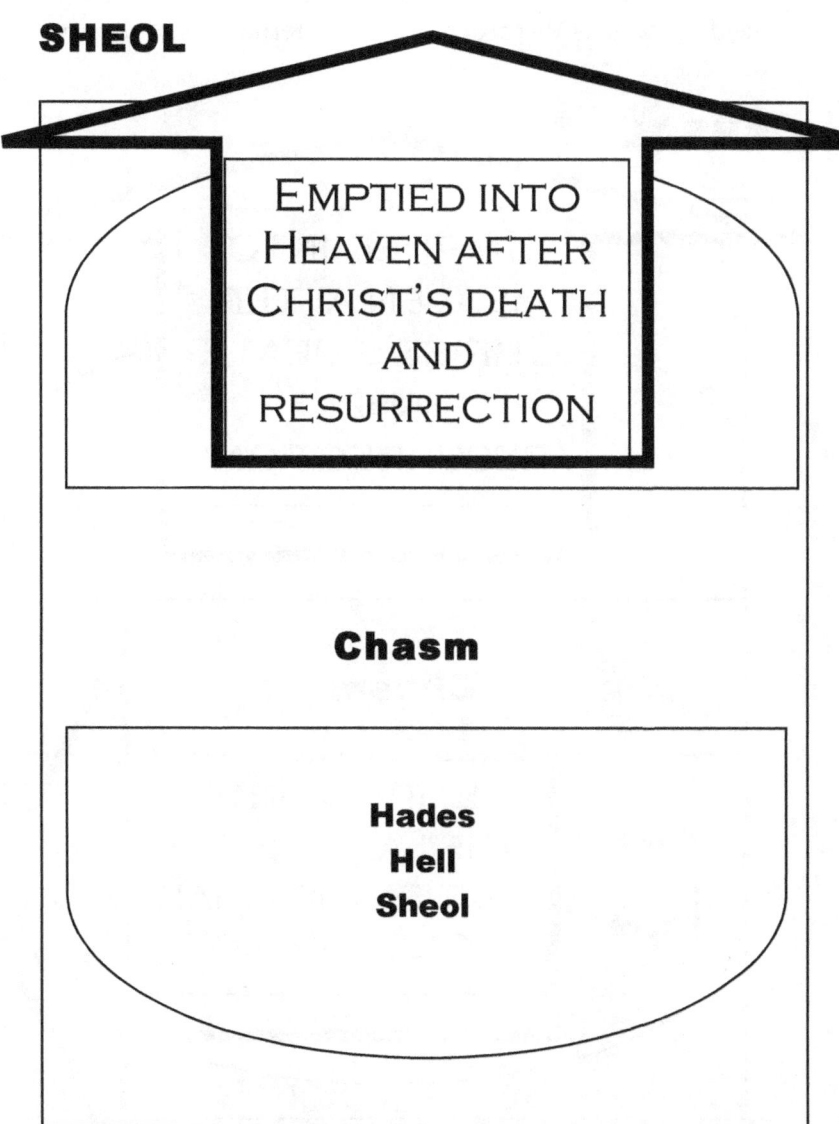

Why There Has To Be A Hell

The future: The future of hell takes place when hell has been emptied of its inhabitants as they face their judgment day and then the temporary storage container, which is hell, along with death, is thrown into the lake of fire (Revelation 20:10-15). Both compartments have been emptied into eternity; and this holding place is no longer needed, so it is discarded into the eternal waste dump -- the lake of fire.

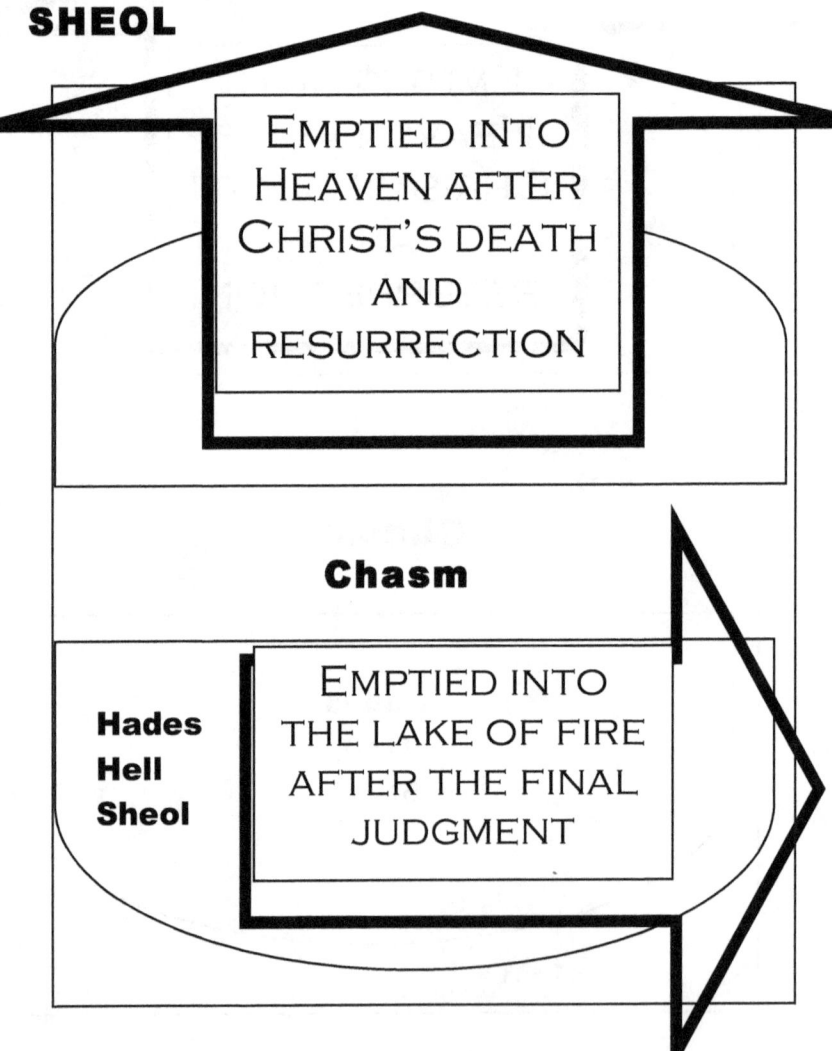

The Future of Hell

There are two primary passages about the future or final destination of hell that are crucial to examine.

The following passage is one of the most extensive passages from the lips of Jesus regarding judgment and the afterlife that begins at the end of the age. These are truths that need to be explored to determine what the nature of the afterlife is. This is unvarnished truth from the Son of God Himself regarding the end of the world. We should pay attention.

WHAT DOES JESUS TELL US ABOUT THE FUTURE OF THE BLESSED AND THE DAMNED IN MATTHEW 25:31-46?

> **Matthew 25:31-46** - *But when the Son of Man comes in His glory, and all the angels with Him, then He will sit on His glorious throne. All the nations will be gathered before Him; and He will separate them from one another, as the shepherd separates the sheep from the goats; and He will put the sheep on His right, and the goats on the left. Then the King will say to those on His right, "Come, you who are blessed of My Father, inherit the kingdom prepared for you from the foundation of the world. For I was hungry, and you gave Me something to eat; I was thirsty, and you gave Me something to drink; I was a stranger, and you invited Me in; naked, and you clothed Me; I was sick, and you visited Me; I was in prison, and you came to Me." Then the righteous will answer Him, "Lord, when did we see You hungry, and feed You, or thirsty, and give You something to drink? And when did we see You a stranger, and invite You in, or naked, and clothe You? When did we see You sick, or in prison, and come to You?" The King will answer and say to them, "Truly I say to you, to the extent that you*

did it to one of these brothers of Mine, even the least of them, you did it to Me." Then He will also say to those on His left, "Depart from Me, accursed ones, into the eternal fire which has been prepared for the devil and his angels; for I was hungry, and you gave Me nothing to eat; I was thirsty, and you gave Me nothing to drink; I was a stranger, and you did not invite Me in; naked, and you did not clothe Me; sick, and in prison, and you did not visit Me." Then they themselves also will answer, "Lord, when did we see You hungry, or thirsty, or a stranger, or naked, or sick, or in prison, and did not take care of You?" Then He will answer them, "Truly I say to you, to the extent that you did not do it to one of the least of these, you did not do it to Me." These will go away into eternal punishment, but the righteous into eternal life.

WHAT HAPPENS AT THE END OF THE AGE?

Jesus is clear as to what happens at the end of the age. He returns in glory surrounded by angels. This is the same picture that is painted by the prophets and the apostles throughout the New Testament.

2 Thessalonians 1:6-10 - *For after all it is only just for God to repay with affliction those who afflict you, and to give relief to you who are afflicted and to us as well when the Lord Jesus will be revealed from heaven with His mighty angels in flaming fire, dealing out retribution to those who do not know God and to those who do not obey the gospel of our Lord Jesus. These will pay the penalty of eternal destruction, away from the presence of the Lord and from the glory of His power, when He comes to be glorified in His saints on that day, and to be marveled at among all who have believed—for our testimony to you was believed.*

Revelation 19:11-16 - *And I saw heaven opened, and behold, a white horse, and He who sat on it is called Faithful and True, and in righteousness He judges and wages war. His eyes are a flame of fire, and on His head are many diadems; and He has a name written on Him, which no one knows except Himself. He is clothed with a robe dipped in blood, and His name is called The Word of God. And the armies, which are in heaven, clothed in fine linen, white and clean, were following Him on white horses. From His mouth comes a sharp sword, so that with it He may strike down the nations, and He will rule them with a rod of iron; and He treads the wine press of the fierce wrath of God, the Almighty. And on His robe and on His thigh He has a name written, "KING OF KINGS, AND LORD OF LORDS."*

His return in glory and majesty is the blessed hope of the church (Titus 2:13). He is coming back, and this time it will be with power and authority not veiled by His gentleness and humility.

One of the features of Christ's second coming is that He will mount His glorious throne. This is clearly a reference to His beginning the judgment of the world. Christ has been established by God the Father as the judge of the world (John 5:26-29). It is this judgment at the end of the age that is in view in this passage. It takes place right after Christ returns and He has established his authority.

All the people of the nations who are still alive will be brought before Christ to be judged by Him. It is in this way that Christ will decide who will go into His kingdom and who will begin the consequences of selfish and unloving actions.

> *All the nations will be gathered before Him; and He will separate them from one another, as the shepherd separates the sheep from the goats; and He will put the sheep on His right, and the goats on the left.*

Christ will begin a separation process for those who will go into His kingdom. There will be some who will be praised for their actions of love, kindness, grace and mercy.

> *Then the King will say to those on His right, "Come, you who are blessed of My Father, inherit the kingdom prepared for you from the foundation of the world. For I was hungry, and you gave Me something to eat; I was thirsty, and you gave Me something to drink; I was a stranger, and you invited Me in; naked, and you clothed Me; I was sick, and you visited Me; I was in prison, and you came to Me."*

And there will be those who will be condemned for their selfish, hoarding, and unloving ways.

> *Then He will also say to those on His left, "Depart from Me, accursed ones, into the eternal fire which has been prepared for the devil and his angels; for I was hungry, and you gave Me nothing to eat; I was thirsty, and you gave Me nothing to drink; I was a stranger, and you did not invite Me in; naked, and you did not clothe Me; sick, and in prison, and you did not visit Me."*

In each case the people who are praised and the people who are condemned will respond that they were not aware that Christ was in the midst of difficulty. It was the heart of love and compassion that Christ was looking for. The condemned group only cared when they saw some gain in it for them: "If we had known it was you then we would have acted." The righteous group allowed their heart of love to flow out to those in need regardless of who it was or when it was. It is this heart of love and selflessness that shows God in the soul of the person. It is God who energizes a person to love beyond any gain for themselves. It is this desire to let the love of God flow through you to others that is commendable.

Realize that the two great commandments (love the Lord your God with all your heart, soul, mind, and strength and your neighbor as yourself) are not religious platitudes but the key evidence of God in your life. We are saved from the wrath of God through faith and not because of our works; but if our faith does not invite Jesus deep enough into our lives and allow Him to actually change us into His agents in the world, then He will declare that He never knew us (Matthew 7:21-23). As the book of James tells us, *Even so faith, if it has no works, is dead, being by itself.* Our faith must allow God to love others through us.

WHAT DO WE LEARN ABOUT THE STATE OF THE BLESSED FROM JESUS' STATEMENTS?

Jesus rewards those who loved Him by loving others by addressing them first. They are blessed and are about to be ushered into His kingdom. He honors them by not making them wait for their inheritance. He embraces them with His words and actions as soon as He has established His authority over the nations of the world.

The great dream of the faithful for thousands of years is to receive an invitation from Christ to be His guest in the kingdom of God the Father. That day of all days is finally here. Those who have allowed their faith to become alive in and through them by actions of love and mercy will be rewarded with this invitation personally from Jesus the King of the world.

Jesus rehearses how their faith in Him became real. They offered him food and drink, clothing and shelter, comfort and encouragement when He was in need. When He prompted them to love, they acted and were ready to enlarge their hearts to pour out the love of God on those who were needy, broken, afflicted, and even undesirable. Jesus does not want these people's actions in the flow of His will to pass without being honored and noticed. Their actions were probably dismissed and even ridiculed at the time. But now the King is remembering and letting everyone know that love is never a wrong action. Kindness and mercy echo throughout eternity.

The people who are being honored for their love and sacrifice were not aware of what they were doing as a love gift to Jesus but were instead just living the way Christ, who lived within them, wanted them to. It is this acting in the right way even though no one notices that gets Jesus' attention. Jesus notices and sees everything. He will reward and honor each and every time His people let Him flow through them. Never forget that. It may be hidden from those around you but it is not hidden from the Almighty God who sees everything we do.

One of the things we must remind ourselves of is that caring for those in need is caring for Jesus. He tells these people that they had loved Him and served Him. They didn't see it that way in their historical moment but instead saw a needy person in front of them. Every day we come across Jesus in these needy states. Sometimes it is someone in our own family who needs a hug or an ear. Sometimes it is a colleague at work who needs some help or some advice. Sometimes it is a homeless person who wants to change or needs some resources to keep going.

WHAT DO WE LEARN ABOUT THE STATE OF THE DAMNED?

The reality of the future is that some people will be damned for their actions and their stubborn refusal to repent of their ways and embrace the forgiveness of God that resides in Jesus. They have chosen a pathway of selfishness and rebellion that will continue to grow within them and requires that they be contained in a damnable place called the eternal fire.

It is clear that those who are condemned to this awful place are those whose love did not reach beyond themselves. They never cared, sacrificed, or met the need of others without some tangible, immediate gain for themselves. It is this selfish love that is damnable. Real love that comes from God escapes the gravity of self. Everyone without the aid of God is capable of selfish love. But that will not build a healthy society and will surely corrupt any community that exists on that basis. Some even believe that one of the hellish features of damnation is that a person will be surrounded by those who only are capable of selfish love.

Jesus must separate those who love selflessly and those who love selfishly. They have been intermixed in the world up to this point. It is this separation that shows fully the kind of person we are. Have we been a person who loves others with no thought of how we might benefit or have we been a person who is always calculating "what's in it for me?" These are not trivial questions. The answer that springs from our hearts shouts to the Lord Jesus whether we will be separated to the right or to the left.

Those who have been separated to the left are spoken to second after the blessed group has been invited into the kingdom. Jesus walks them through their lifestyle and their values as exhibited by their refusal to love when it was beyond their self-interest. It is entirely possible that this exchange that takes only a few sentences here is really a summary statement for an individual process of review conducted mentally with each person. Jesus walks with the person through their life, looking for times when they loved without personal gain. When He finds none, He concludes with them that He was not a part of their life in any meaningful way. It is their selfishness and refusal to embrace the forgiveness and power of Christ that seals their fate. They refuse God's power. They refuse God's escape route. They chose to embrace themselves rather than God. They have erected a monument to themselves through their choices, actions, and words.

Jesus, after their review, renders judgment. They will be banished to eternal fire.

> **Matthew 25:41** - *Then He will also say to those on His left, "Depart from Me, accursed ones, into the eternal fire which has been prepared for the devil and his angels."*

Whatever this fire is and however it works, it is an eternal thing and they are in it eternally. He does not say that they will only be there for a few moments until they are consumed. He states, in a matter-of-fact manner, that they will be present in eternal fire.

We know from our observations about Jesus' comments in Luke 16:19-26 that eternal fire does not restrict conversation; it does not retard movement; it does not keep a person from trying to get out of its affliction; and it does not change an arrogant attitude and a core self-focus. The rich man in the story from Luke was doing all of these things while being in the midst of eternal fire. He does testify that he is in agony and torment, but he can still do all these other things.

The question is whether the fire is eternal and the people are not or the people and fire are eternal which is why the fire must be eternal. Is the soul of a person eternal? Jesus' answer is that the soul of humanity is eternal. Their actions, choices, and words ripple on forever and they do also as conscious beings. Notice that he states that the people who are ushered into eternal fire are ushered into eternal punishment.

These will go away into eternal punishment, but the righteous into eternal life.

The only way a person could be in eternal punishment is if they were still in the punishment. It is no longer punishment if they are not there. It seems to me that the two biggest problems with our understanding eternal fire and eternal punishment are our preconceived ideas about fire and about eternity. Both of these will be dealt with in the next chapter.

It is interesting that Jesus tells us that this toxic waste dump of eternal fire was not designed for humans but for the Devil and his angels. This place called eternal punishment and eternal fire was designed for the rebel angels. It is strong enough to hold them in some kind of containment field. It also holds individual people who have rejected God's offer of forgiveness.

WHAT DO THE DAMNED DECLARE ABOUT THEIR LOVE?

Those who are damned because their love was selfish at its core protest the judgment that has been rendered against them. But their words only prove more surely that they have a selfish point of view.

> Then they themselves also will answer, "Lord, when did we see You hungry, or thirsty, or a stranger, or naked, or sick, or in prison, and did not take care of You?"

Their protest confirms their self-focus. If we had known it was **YOU** we would have treated **YOU** differently. Everything in their life attaches to a "How do I maximize my win here?" Jesus sees through the façade of love and care to expose the self-seeking: "If someone who is important or could help me is in trouble, then it is worth it for me to help them. But if there is no obvious way that I would benefit from helping, then I will not."

HOW LONG DOES THE STATE OF THE BLESSED LAST?

Eternity!!! It has been the happy and anticipated joy of every Christian believer that they will be in heaven for eternity. Jesus states this is so:

> **Matthew 25:34** - *Then the King will say to those on His right, "Come, you who are blessed of My Father, inherit the kingdom prepared for you from the foundation of the world."*

Technically Jesus promises those who obey Him and act on the impulse to meet the needs of those around them will inherit the kingdom prepared before the foundation of the world. It is an eternal kingdom. It dwells outside of time and space. We live in a time-based universe, so we have injected our ideas of time onto our understanding of eternity when really eternity is timeless. It is the eternal now. Scholars tell us that eternity is the possession of all the moments at once and that there is no passage of time in eternity; it is always now.

How long do the damned stay in the place of the damned?

Jesus states clearly that those who are condemned for their selfish lack of love are being sent to eternal fire and eternal punishment. This clearly indicates that the soul of each person is immortal or eternal. There is no mention of their soul being consumed in the eternal fire. Instead, Jesus explains the concept in a different manner by saying that these people who are condemned will be punished eternally.

It is again important to state that our problem with eternal punishment is that we do not understand eternity. We think of eternity as endless blocks of time rammed one against another forever. But eternity in the Judeo and Christian sense is timeless. Eternity is the constant now. It is the embrace of all the moments at once. God does not experience time as a flow of moments beneath Him. Instead He enjoys all the moments at once and continually. It is like the person who sits in the control tower and watches the whole parade at the same time rather than interacting with each float or band as it goes by. He is eternal, the everlasting one. Because of our inadequate understanding of eternity, some have concluded that heaven will get boring. Anything that goes on forever will be devoid of meaning after awhile. This is the way it is in our finite lives and many project this upon eternity. The answer to the question, "How long does heaven last?" It lasts one eternal moment! The answer to the question, "How long does hell last?" It lasts one eternal moment! When we step into eternity we enter a completely different experience. It is outside of time.

Some have chosen to diminish the power and equivalence of the words of Jesus about eternal punishment and eternal life by having eternal mean something different than eternal. But Jesus was especially clear. If we treasure the concept that those who have been forgiven for their sins will enjoy eternal life, then we cannot eviscerate his words that those who reject His offer of forgiveness will face eternal punishment. If heaven is eternal and people don't graduate out of it, then hell and the lake of fire are eternal and people don't graduate out of there either. Yes, it is eternal destruction, but they are not destroyed so as to not exist.

The prophet Daniel does the same equivalence between heaven and hell that Jesus does in this passage:

Daniel 12:2 - *Many of those who sleep in the dust of the ground will awake, these to everlasting life, but the others to disgrace and everlasting contempt.*

Notice that Daniel equates everlasting life with everlasting contempt. Both require a receiver to have meaning. One cannot be given everlasting life if one is not present to receive it. On the other side, one cannot be subject to everlasting contempt unless one is present to receive it. Humanity has an eternal soul. It was built for eternity and it will be eternal. Every human being's choices, actions, words, and motives are subject to huge consequences. The testimony of Scripture is that all have turned aside; no one seeks for God and no one understands (Romans 3:10-12). Everyone is headed to eternal punishment. And yet God so loved these eternal creatures that He created that He sent His only begotten Son that whosoever believes in Him will not perish but shall have everlasting life. Eternity will swallow us one day when the veil of this life is over. It will swallow some into life and some into death.

WHAT DOES JESUS NOT TELL US?

Sometimes it is very instructive to look at what a passage doesn't say. What answers are not given to the obvious questions? Jesus is telling us of the nature of judgment and its consequences. He does not suggest that the position of the condemned is temporary. There is not within the words "eternal fire; nor eternal punishment" any hint that after a few millennia it will end.

Jesus also does not say that this awful place of consequences and punishment is really the imaginative work of religious zealots trying to control people's lives for their gain. No, He states plainly and simply that this awful place of eternal punishment exists and people would do well to aim at faith in God and love from God so that they should escape that place.

Finally, Jesus does not say that after the judgment of people there is a work release program which will allow a person to work off their sins and get out of eternal fire after so long. The idea of purification for one's own sins through work and good behavior does not come from the lips of Jesus. It may seem like a great idea to human imagination, but Jesus doesn't mention it. He talks about eternal consequences for choices, actions, and words here on earth.

Jesus shoots straight with us about the way life really is. He tells us in the Sermon on the Mount that being humble and meek is better than being proud and aggressive. We don't want to believe Him, but He is right. He tells us that doing religious rituals to impress our religious friends is a waste. He also tells us that there is a real hell and eventually a real place of eternal fire. Jesus says that these are real places. There is a heaven to gain and a hell to lose. If we are to embrace Jesus as Lord and God, then we must agree with what He says about the landscape of eternity even if it does not agree with our conception of what ought to be.

What do we learn from Revelations 20:10-15 about the nature of hell?

Examine the following passage for yourself and then join me in a brief overview of the dominating truths from this passage:

> **Revelation 20:10-15 -** *And the devil who deceived them was thrown into the lake of fire and brimstone, where the beast and the false prophet are also; and they will be tormented day and night forever and ever. Then I saw a great white throne and Him who sat upon it, from whose presence earth and heaven fled away, and no place was found for them. And I saw the dead, the great and the small, standing before the throne, and books were opened; and another book was opened, which is the book of life; and the dead were judged from the things which were written in the books, according to their deeds. And the sea gave up the dead which were in it, and death and Hades gave up the dead which were in them; and they were judged, every one of them according to their deeds. Then death and Hades were thrown into the lake of fire. This is the second death, the lake of fire. And if anyone's name was not found written in the book of life, he was thrown into the lake of fire.*

What do we learn about the devil from this passage?

We learn that there is a spiritual being who is bent on humanity's enslavement and destruction and has been and will be at work to deceive people about the real purpose of life. We learn that this being called the Devil in this passage will be judged and thrown into a lake of fire where two other human beings have already been assigned and where he (the Devil) will experience eternal torment.

Another misconception about the Devil, hell, and the lake of fire is that somehow the Devil runs the place. This is not the case. He and his minions are what this containment field was originally designed for. He is contained and encased by the lake of fire. He is a prisoner there, not the one who is the ruler of the underworld.

WHAT DO WE LEARN ABOUT JUDGMENT DAY FROM THIS PASSAGE?

We learn that after the Devil is judged and confined into the lake of fire, God will set up a final judgment process. All the records will be opened on every person who has ever lived. These records will be examined. People will be examined based upon their deeds -- what they have done or not done. Every single person who has ever lived will be evaluated by God. There is a second set of records that will also be checked on each person. This is called the Book of Life. If a person is recorded in the Book of Life they are not judged according to their deeds, and they do not end up in the lake of fire. They have passed out of that judgment and into a different type of judgment. Another part of Scripture calls this other judgment, the judgment seat of Christ (2 Corinthians 5:10).

We understand from another part of Scripture that sincere trust and faith in the life, death, and resurrection of Jesus Christ as your only deeds of merit cause a person to be recorded in the Book of Life and bound for a heaven that they do not deserve (Romans 10:9,10; John 3:16).

WHAT DO WE LEARN ABOUT HELL FROM THIS PASSAGE?

After God's evaluation of every single person and their assignment to heaven or hell, then death (the separation of a person's soul from their body) and hell (the abode of the dead during the history of our world) will be thrown into the lake of fire as the permanent exclamation of the end of this world. The lake of fire and what it does is given a new title because of what it does. It is called the second death. If the first death is the separation of a person's soul from their body, then the second death would most likely be the separation of a person from the grace of God.

One of the great problems with our understanding, or may I say misunderstanding, of hell is that people have left the biblical data behind and tried to deal with the reality of hell from their own creative imaginations. The visions of hell when Scripture is no longer the source material can become bizarre. As Alice Turner states:

> The landscape of Hell is the largest shared construction project in imaginative history, and its chief architects have been creative giants, Homer, Virgil, Plato, Augustine, Dante, Bosch, Michelangelo, Milton, Goeth, Blake and more.[2]

Chapter 4
Part I

Why Does There Have To Be A Hell?

Mark Twain is reported to have said, "It is not the parts of the Bible that I don't understand that trouble me. It is the parts of the Bible that I do understand that trouble me the most."

The doctrine of hell is one of those doctrines. Scripture presents this as a place of containment for the Devil, his angels, and the departed wicked as well as a place of ultimate justice with no escape.

Stop

There may be a temptation to skip the first few chapters of this book and jump to the reasons why there must be a hell but do not do that. If you are reading this section without reading the first three chapters, this section will not make as much sense to you. It is important that you work through what Jesus says and grapple with His words. It is His words and His ideas that are full of grace and truth. Start with the first chapter on "What Does Jesus Tell Us About Hell."

Then proceed to "The Architecture of Hell" and then "The Future of Hell." This will allow you to have a sufficient background to grapple with this section on "Why There Has to be a Hell." When you spend enough time with what Jesus says, a different perspective will emerge. You will find yourself ready to receive the truth of hell presented in the other chapters. If you jump to the reasons for hell, then this book will become just one more philosophical discussion or intellectual game on the subject of hell.

STOP

Because of Scripture's clarity on the afterlife and hell in particular, some have sought to re-interpret our understanding of hell so it doesn't seem so terrible. There are a number of teachers and intellectuals who want hell to go away as a truth. They try and ignore it, ridicule it, or attack it so its existence does not seem so threatening.

Some think that we have the right to start from ourselves and dream up what God should do in this present existence and in the afterlife. However, He has clearly told us what He will do to us in the afterlife and what the rules are that govern our place there. It is what God says that we must deal with, not what we would want Him to do. Some conclude that hell doesn't make sense to them so there is no reason why God should have one. It escapes their notice that there are many things that God knows that they do not and that they are incapable of comprehending. The Bible is full of truth that we need to know even if a particular period of time or a particular culture cannot appreciate that truth. Listen to J.P.

Mooreland discuss the recent rejection of the doctrine of hell based upon cultural conditioning:

> It is wrong to think God is simply a loving being, especially if you mean loving in the sense that most Americans use that word today. Yes, God is a compassionate being, but He is also just, moral, and pure being. So God's decisions are not based on modern, American sentimentalism. This is one of the reasons why people have never had a difficult time with the idea of hell until modern times. People today tend to care only for the softer virtues like love and tenderness, while they've forgotten the hard virtues of holiness, righteousness, and justice.[1]

It would be lovely if God allowed us to eliminate anything we don't like or change anything we don't understand, but that is not the way it is.

A distortion is clearly at work in western civilization. Our culture presently has a strong bias as to what sounds right to us in a materialistic, naturalistic, secular culture. This cultural filter does not allow us to embrace the truths that were easy for other cultures and peoples to embrace. We find it hard to imagine a God who is loving and capable of condemning people to eternal hell over transgressions that we do not consider all that heinous. We consider adultery as almost inconsequential, stealing as the nature of work and life, and lying as tact. We are a culture that abhors pain of any kind; and therefore we cannot abide the truth that those who choose a self-focused, selfish life will be in pain for eternity because of their choices. We see the ultimate evil as pain. God, instead, sees the destruction of sinfulness. Every sin creates great amounts of destruction that our culture hides from us.

Why There Has To Be A Hell

Think of the cultures that allow and even condone selling children into sexual slavery. These cultures have come to the place where they do not see this as destructive and wrong but instead necessary and even honorable. In many cases it is almost impossible for them to understand that this is a wrong action. In much the same way all cultures have embraced actions and habits that are outside the boundaries of the Ten Commandments and are wrong in the eyes of God, but they cannot see it that way because their culture tells them it is right.

We are appalled that the Bible suggests that a person will be condemned forever for what our culture has come to view as inconsequential actions. This cannot be. Many imagine a Supreme Being who reasons similar to how they do. The Almighty God cannot reason so different from how I reason. But He does and He shows us His reasoning in the Bible.

There is power in truth. Decisions become crystal clear when you finally know the truth, unless you choose to play the fool. If you come to a Y in the road and wonder what to do, it becomes clear which way to turn if you know that down one road you will find a huge hole that will wreck your car and leave you stranded. You know not to go that way. When you know that smoking cigarettes will most likely cut between twenty to thirty years off your life, it becomes clear that you should not smoke. When you know that alcohol is a poison to the human body that always damages the body and, in some people, becomes an addictive substance, it is clear that you should not drink alcohol. In the same way the truth about hell allows for correct decisions.

The truth of the matter is that there is an eternal place of justice called hell and eventually the lake of fire where those who violate God's laws and live lives of selfishness and rebellion are exiled. The only exception is for those who realize their folly, repent, and throw themselves on the mercy of God. God has promised to pardon all those who sincerely plead for His mercy because of what He accomplished through the life, death, and resurrection of Jesus of Nazareth, the Christ.

Hell is a fact of human existence. It is a sobering fact, an awful fact; but it is still a fact. It is a place that has to exist for a number of reasons. Let me briefly go over some of the reasons. We will explore each of these in more detail later in this chapter.

1) Hell exists because there is a need for justice.

2) Hell exists because people will last forever.

3) Hell exists because people's choices count forever.

4) Hell exists because sin needs to be contained.

5) Hell exists because selfishness grows even after death.

6) Hell exists because of the butterfly effects of sin.

7) Hell exists because God is omniscient and unchanging.

8) Hell exists because there is a hierarchical order of being.

9) Hell exists because of the point of no return.

10) Hell exists because Christian authorities say it does.

WHY DOES THERE HAVE TO BE A HELL?

Let's put what we have seen from the crucial passages of Scripture together with other key passages of Scripture and construct a preliminary list of the reasons why God would create and sustain a place we call hell and the lake of fire. In each of these reasons we will examine the basic rationale for this reason. Whole books have been and need to be written on these issues.

1. **Hell exists because there is a need for a place of ultimate justice for the people of this world.**

   Human beings all over the world believe in life after death, in the survival of the conscious personality after the body has ceased to function. Anthropologists, archaeologists, sociologists, classicists, and analysts of the history of comparative religions agree that this is true of all cultures, so far as we know.[2]

   The truth of hell resides within every culture. The idea of an afterlife cannot be ignored because we cannot take a day trip there and take samples. There is a need for justice beyond any level of justice that has been and can be meted out here on earth. Some escape the earthly justice that they are due, but deep inside our being there is the idea and the cry for an eternal justice. The atrocities that are committed in this life require an ultimate judge and an ultimate judgment.

   There is a need for a place of ultimate justice for the people of this world. Will evil ever be fully recompensed? If a person escapes justice here in this life, we have surety that they will not escape justice in the next life. Too often Christians are ashamed of hell when it should be a rallying cry. The fact that everyone is headed to a personal review of their actions, choices, and words where absolute justice will be meted out should motivate Christians to get the word out that no one needs to face this pure form of justice. We should be motivated to get the word out that because of God's great love, all of the justice that should be heaped upon us has been heaped upon Christ at the cross. The eternal God took on flesh so that He could take away the sins of the world (John 1:29). Look at what the Scripture says in **Romans 2:5-10:**

> *But because of your stubbornness and unrepentant heart you are storing up wrath for yourself in the day of wrath and revelation of the righteous judgment of God, who WILL RENDER TO EACH PERSON ACCORDING TO HIS DEEDS: to those who by perseverance in doing good seek for glory and honor and immortality, eternal life; but to those who are selfishly ambitious and do not obey the truth, but obey unrighteousness, wrath and indignation. There will be tribulation and distress for every soul of man who does evil, of the Jew first and also of the Greek, but glory and honor and peace to everyone who does good, to the Jew first and also to the Greek.*

Because people will last forever, we should plead with them to be reconciled to God. It is clear from Jesus' words in Matthew 25 that mankind has an eternal soul.

> *Then He will also say to those on His left, "Depart from Me, accursed ones, into the eternal fire which has been prepared for the devil and his angels."*

> *These will go away into eternal punishment, but the righteous into eternal life.*

We are so unaccustomed to real justice that it seems shocking to us when it is meted out. Ezekiel 18:4: *Behold, all souls are Mine; the soul of the father as well as the soul of the son is Mine. The soul who sins will die.* Look what God tells

Adam and Eve in the garden in Genesis 2:16, 17: *The LORD God commanded the man, saying, "From any tree of the garden you may eat freely; but from the tree of the knowledge of good and evil you shall not eat, for in the day that you eat from it you will surely die."*

Throughout the Scriptures God delivers justice to various individuals. Why would we think that God will not bring about justice on those who continue to rebel against His rule over their lives? Notice just some of the justice meted out in Scripture. Adam and Eve are driven out of the garden. Cain is made to wander among his relatives with only a special mark to protect him from his extended family's vengeance for the murder of Abel. All of the people of Noah's day perish in the flood for their sinful ways. The Israelites who rebelled against God in the desert were swallowed by the earth. Ananias and Sapphira perished immediately after being confronted about their lies to God.

2. Hell exists because people will last forever; they have an eternal soul.

Once one steps into eternity, one steps into timelessness. The flow of time has no meaning and no movement. Our concept of eternal hell is still too wrapped up in our materialistic understanding of death as "ceasing to be" and our conception of time as a "succession of moments."

This is really the ultimate argument for the eternality of hell. If the Bible states that the soul is eternal or will last forever as a conscious being, then there is no question that hell must be eternal. If the soul of every human is eternal and cannot be ultimately or completely destroyed, then hell becomes the container to hold these immortals who choose poorly. The question then becomes: Are there verses that suggest that the soul is immortal and cannot be destroyed?

Look at the following verses and their insistence that heaven and hell are eternal. The Scriptures are unequivocal about the nature of the afterlife; it is eternal.

Revelation 20:10 - *And the devil who deceived them was thrown into the lake of fire and brimstone, where the beast and the false prophet are also; and <u>they will be tormented day and night forever and ever</u>.*

We learn at least three things about the eternality of the soul from this passage. First, the Devil who is an eternal spiritual being will be tormented day and night forever and ever by being placed in the lake of fire. This place will clearly be a place of containment, judgment, and punishment for this being that will continue to exist and would do his work again if he were allowed to escape that place.

The second thing that we learn from this passage about the eternality of the soul is that two human associates (the Beast and the False Prophet) of the Devil have already been condemned to the lake of fire. They are also said to be tormented day and night forever and ever. How is this possible? It is because they have an eternal soul that will not be ultimately and finally destroyed in whatever containment, judgment, and punishment is a part of the lake of fire.

The third fact from this passage is that all three of these individuals -- one angelic and two human -- will experience perpetual torment for their actions. They must exist for this punishment, containment, and judgment to continue perpetually. Since both angelic and human entities are said to experience eternal torment, then the souls of both must be eternal.

This containment field in eternity is within the view of the eternal city (Revelation 21:8; 22:15). The fact that the Bible does not flinch away from this truth would suggest that there is something in our culture that does not allow us to see this as a reasonable outcome for the wicked. We have become culturally and emotionally unable to look at this truth.

We might like it to be different but it isn't. Only facing facts squarely will allow us to build an adequate worldview. Some have argued for a limited immortality. It is possible that it is true, but God has given us no solid clues that humans have only limited immortality. Because most today do not have a real appreciation for the need for justice, we find ourselves wanting to limit the duration, purpose, or intensity of hell. Just because we don't want there to be a hell doesn't wish it away. This is often an emotional game of denial. If the Scriptures are the true guide to faith and life, then we must take what it says and grapple with these facts. We are appalled by the idea of endless blocks of time being slammed one against another with the individual in torment, but what if that is the wrong picture of eternity. We are even appalled at the idea of endless blocks of time spent in heaven. It all sounds like too much. We would rather just cease to exist.

One of the interesting verses that strongly declares the eternality of the soul is Revelation 22:15. Notice the present tense verbs and continuing practices of evil.

> **Revelation 22:15** *Outside are the dogs and the sorcerers and the immoral persons and the murderers and the idolaters, and everyone who loves and practices lying.*

Notice in this verse that those who are in the lake of fire -- who exist outside of the heavenly city -- are said to still exist. There is no past tense to their existence. The verse does not read that outside *were* the dogs and the sorcerers; they are *still there* outside the heavenly gates. Notice also that God tells us that those who love and practice lying are still lying; the practice continues. The corruption of their soul is continuing.

Annihilationism comes from a materialistic point of view (physical elements and physical existence is all there is). If we have an eternal soul, then something must be done with it if it becomes toxic just like spent fuel rods from nuclear reactors have to be stored for thousands of years after only a few months of use.

You can't just destroy an eternal soul. God's word says so. It is eternal and it should become a lover of God, others, and self. Not just a lover of self. If that soul does not orient itself towards God's righteousness, it will be an active agent of unrighteousness. It is only with God's grace that a person can become a lover of God, but God's grace is available. We are an eternal soul whether we want to be or not; so choose wisely. "If you hear His voice, do not harden your heart."

Let us continue to examine Scripture for its position on the eternality of the soul.

> **Daniel 12:2** - *Many of those who sleep in the dust of the ground will awake, these to **everlasting life**, but the others to disgrace and **everlasting contempt**.*

Notice the use of the word *everlasting* in this verse. It is used both of heaven and of hell. Those who are invited into heaven are given everlasting life and those who are assigned to hell are given everlasting contempt. Everlasting is the same word in both cases. If heaven is everlasting positive consciousness, then the second everlasting must be of the same sort of dimensionality. It is not possible to have one everlasting mean one thing and then seven words later the same word to mean temporary.

Look at these verses that speak to this issue of the eternality of the soul:

> **Matthew 25:41-46** - *Then He will also say to those on His left, "<u>Depart from Me, accursed ones, into the eternal fire which has been prepared for the devil and his angels;</u> for I was hungry, and you gave Me nothing to eat; I was thirsty, and you gave Me nothing to drink; I was a stranger, and you did not invite Me in; naked, and you did not clothe Me; sick, and in prison, and you did not visit Me." Then they themselves also will answer, "Lord, when did we see You hungry, or thirsty, or a stranger, or naked, or sick, or in prison, and did not take care of You?" Then He will answer them, "Truly I say to you, to the extent that you did not do it to one of the least of these, you did not do it to Me." <u>These will go away into eternal punishment, but the righteous into eternal life.</u>*

Notice that eternal punishment and eternal life are directly parallel. If one is forever then the other is forever. Secondly, if the punishment is eternal then doesn't the soul that is being punished have to be eternal? Thirdly, the fire is eternal and there is little point in having eternal fire for a group of finite beings, so it is safe to say that the beings are eternal.

One of the key ideas that emerges from this discussion about eternal life and eternal punishment is why would God make our souls eternal. The answer is best understood as that in order for the finite to enjoy any type of relationship with God, we must have an eternal aspect to us. That is our soul.

In the Bible Hell is separation or banishment from the most beautiful being in the world – God himself. It is exclusion from anything that matters, from all value, not only from God but also from those who have come to know and love him.[3]

Hell is the final sentence that says you refused regularly to live for the purpose for which you were made, and the only alternative is to sentence you away for all eternity. So it is a punishment. But it is the natural consequence of a life that has been lived in a certain direction.[4]

Our problem with eternity.

One of the greatest problems with understanding hell is our present conception of time. We have only experienced time as a linear concept flowing in one direction. This linear experience of time is what we assume when we think of hell being eternal. We perceive endless blocks of time being slammed one next to the other without end, and we rightly see this as a very difficult concept for a just God. Interestingly many people have the same problem with heaven being eternal. Many assume that they will get bored with heaven after eons of time no matter how good it is. Eternity and God are outside of our limited time dimensions.

But it is our conception of time that is all wrong, not the eternality of hell or heaven. Eternity is not measured in terms of its length of time. Eternity is the eternal now. The Bible presents a different picture of eternity than our present time conceptions. When you are in eternity there is no past, present or future; it is just now. There is some debate among theologians and philosophers as to whether eternity is timeless or multi-dimensional in its orientation to time. But both sides agree that to be in eternity means that we are beyond one-dimensional time boundaries.

What do these verses suggest about the nature of time and eternity?

Exodus 3:14 - *God said to Moses, "I AM WHO I AM"; and He said, "Thus you shall say to the sons of Israel, I AM has sent me to you."*

This verse tells us of God's description of Himself as the living verb to be. I AM is His personal name. He is eternity and the ever living, ever present One. When we go to be with Him, He is inviting us into eternity and into the constant now.

Revelation 21:23 - *And the city has no need of the sun or of the moon to shine on it, for the glory of God has illumined it, and its lamp is the Lamb.*

The old measurements of time will cease to be needed. There will be no rotation of the earth around a star. There will be no moon to mark the night when we should rest. The whole of time will be different because it will be eternity and not linear time as it was here on earth.

Revelation 22:5 - *And there will no longer be any night; and they will not have need of the light of a lamp nor the light of the sun, because the Lord God will illumine them; and they will reign forever and ever.*

For us when we say that hell will be forever, this seems like too long of a time. We cannot comprehend forever from our time references. We have the wrong idea of time in eternity because we only experience one dimension of time in one direction. We have never experienced time in any other way than a linear experience in one direction. Therefore it is reasonable to conclude that we are conditioned to a one-dimensional orientation to time. It is hard for us to imagine a new and completely different orientation to time other than sequential moments flowing beneath us with no ability to move backward or deeper into any individual moment.

There have been, over the centuries of Christian thought, various approaches to understanding eternity and God with relation to time. Most have come to see that God is timeless and eternity is timeless. In other words, God and eternity are beyond time and space. Some other Christians have seen God and eternity as hyper-dimensional levels of time and space. For illustration purposes we can grow in our understanding of eternity by exploring a multi-dimensional approach to time. I am not necessarily endorsing eternity as a multi-dimensional state but just helping us expand our thinking of eternity beyond our present time constraints.

Scientists tell us that there are hyperspaces (dimensions above length, width, height), so it is possible to surmise that there are dimensions of time above our linear experience of it. Let's think about time in the same way that we think about length, width, and height. We currently only experience length of time, but it is reasonable to conclude that there may be also width and height of time or dimensions of time that are above, beyond, or perpendicular to our time dimension. If time can be conceived of this way, then a multi-dimensional approach to time gives a whole different expansion to our understanding of time in eternity. Eternity is not endless blocks of time but dwelling in time with an ability to move in all directions within a space called time.

Let me give you a stretched illustration to help you see this. If we only experienced one dimension of space, it would be like we were asked to live on a tightrope or a thin board -- a two-by-four. We would live by making our way along this two-by-four. We would be very constrained by the lack of width on the two-by-four and the unidirectional constant movement along the two-by-four. This is the way we feel about time; we just keep moving along this thin ribbon of our existence. We would love to experience other people's moments of time, but we are constrained to our own. And we can only experience their moments when they actually join us in our moments. There is no ability to see or experience others' moments that are different from ours except at a separate time along our own ribbon of experience. Because of the nature of two-by-four, we naturally ask how long is the two-by-four? When do we make it to the end? But if instead of only one dimension of space and if our dimensions of space were opened up to three dimensions, then the same two-by-four could become a series of parallel two-by-fours and walls and a ceiling. What was in one dimension a path, a track, a narrow way would become in a three-dimensional space, a room or house to dwell in. If this were to happen, we would stop asking how long is the two-by-four, and we would begin experiencing all the two-by-fours and all the rooms. We would even be able to go outside of the house. We would experience the three-dimensional house completely differently than we existed on the two-by-four. In just the same way, it is possible that in eternity we will not constantly be asking how long does it last but we will just dwell in it – it will be the eternal present. When we enter eternity we will be swallowed up by a completely different level of time or timelessness itself. The length of heaven and/or hell is irrelevant. It will be like worrying about how long the two-by-fours in the house are. How long will a person be in heaven or hell? One moment -- one glorious moment or one damned moment. Eternity is the eternal now, not a succession of endless minutes.

Why Does There Have To Be A Hell - Part 1

___Time as we know it _____
Past   Future

↑ Time flowing vertically

___Time as we know it _____
Past   Future

Time flowing vertically ↑

___Time as we know it _____
Past   Future ↘ Time flowing in depth

Time as a space to dwell in

If these ideas have any merit, then time becomes a place to dwell instead of a tightrope to make our way along. This is certainly more in keeping with the eternity mentioned in the Bible. This idea of time becoming a place certainly gives a fuller picture of eternity than just one dimension of time. The robustness of the descriptions of God, heaven, and eternity suggests that eternity has many surprises for us -- maybe including hyper-time or some version of timelessness.

Some have also used the recent movie *Inception* as an interesting metaphor for time within time within time flowing at different rates. In this movie the characters are able to enter dreams and manipulate matter and experience different rates of time. They are even able to dream within dreams of dreams. This idea gives us another way of perceiving time beyond our linear, unidirectional, and limited view of time.

What evidence of this timelessness or hyper-dimensional nature to eternity do we have? Well, the spirit world discussed in the Scripture is clearly a part of a hyper-dimensional reality that is above, beyond, and yet connected to our three-dimensional existence here in this life. We see Elisha call upon God to open the eyes of his servant Gehazi so that he may see the multiple creatures that inhabit this hyper-dimensional reality (**2 Kings 6:11-19**):

> *Now the heart of the king of Aram was enraged over this thing; and he called his servants and said to them, "Will you tell me which of us is for the king of Israel?" One of his servants said, "No, my lord, O king; but Elisha, the prophet who is in Israel, tells the king of Israel the words that you speak in your bedroom." So he said, "Go and see where he is, that I may send and take him." And it was told him, saying, "Behold, he is in Dothan." He sent horses and chariots and a great army there, and they*

came by night and surrounded the city. Now when the attendant of the man of God had risen early and gone out, behold, an army with horses and chariots was circling the city. And his servant said to him, "Alas, my master! What shall we do?" So he answered, "Do not fear, for those who are with us are more than those who are with them." Then Elisha prayed and said, "O LORD, I pray, open his eyes that he may see." And the LORD opened the servant's eyes and he saw; and behold, the mountain was full of horses and chariots of fire all around Elisha. When they came down to him, Elisha prayed to the LORD and said, "Strike this people with blindness, I pray." So He struck them with blindness according to the word of Elisha. Then Elisha said to them, "This is not the way, nor is this the city; follow me and I will bring you to the man whom you seek." And he brought them to Samaria.*

We understand that God is a being that dwells on an infinite dimensional plane in which one being can have three distinct persons (**Matthew 28:18-20**):

And Jesus came up and spoke to them, saying, "All authority has been given to Me in heaven and on earth. Go therefore and make disciples of all the nations, baptizing them in the name of the Father and the Son and the Holy Spirit, teaching them to observe all that I commanded you; and lo, I am with you always, even to the end of the age."

The new heavens and the new earth do not mark time through the cycles of the sun but are illuminated by the glory of God and the Lamb (**Revelation 21:23; 22:5**):

And the city has no need of the sun or of the moon to shine on it, for the glory of God has illumined it, and its lamp is the Lamb.

And there will no longer be any night; and they will not have need of the light of a lamp nor the light of the sun, because the Lord God will illumine them; and they will reign forever and ever.

The prophets are not only told what will take place in the future but also are told what could take place in multiple possible futures (**2 Kings 9:1-10**):

Now Elisha the prophet called one of the sons of the prophets and said to him, "Gird up your loins, and take this flask of oil in your hand and go to Ramoth-gilead. When you arrive there, search out Jehu the son of Jehoshaphat the son of Nimshi, and go in and bid him arise from among his brothers, and bring him to an inner room. Then take the flask of oil and pour it on his head and say, 'Thus says the LORD, "I have anointed you king over Israel." Then open the door and flee and do not wait." So the young man, the servant of the prophet, went to Ramoth-gilead. When he came, behold, the captains of the army were sitting, and he said, "I have a word for you, O captain." And Jehu said, "For which one of us?" And he said, "For you, O captain." He arose and went into the house, and he poured the oil on his head and said to him, Thus says the LORD, the God of Israel, "I have anointed you king over the people of the LORD, even over Israel. You shall strike the house of Ahab your master, that I may avenge the blood of My servants the prophets, and the blood of all the servants of the LORD, at the hand of Jezebel. For the whole house of Ahab shall perish, and I will cut off from Ahab every male person both bond and free in Israel. I will make the house of Ahab like the house of Jeroboam the son of Nebat, and like the house of Baasha the son of Ahijah. 'The dogs shall eat Jezebel in the territory of Jezreel, and none shall bury her." Then he opened the door and fled.

Why Does There Have To Be A Hell - Part 1

Elisha sees a glimpse of a possible future that seems impossible at the time he sees it (**2 Kings 7:1**):

> *Then Elisha said, "Listen to the word of the LORD; thus says the LORD, 'Tomorrow about this time a measure of fine flour will be sold for a shekel, and two measures of barley for a shekel, in the gate of Samaria.' "*

Jesus, going outside of our time and even logical dimensions, predicts what would have happened if certain miracles had been done in Sodom and Gomorrah. He is speaking of eternal time and knowledge references and not linear ones (**Matthew 11:20-24**):

> *Then He began to denounce the cities in which most of His miracles were done, because they did not repent. "Woe to you, Chorazin! Woe to you, Bethsaida! For if the miracles had occurred in Tyre and Sidon which occurred in you, they would have repented long ago in sackcloth and ashes. Nevertheless I say to you, it will be more tolerable for Tyre and Sidon in the day of judgment than for you. And you, Capernaum, will not be exalted to heaven, will you? You will descend to Hades; for if the miracles had occurred in Sodom which occurred in you, it would have remained to this day. Nevertheless I say to you that it will be more tolerable for the land of Sodom in the day of judgment, than for you."*

He is displaying the omniscience of God, knowing all the possibilities of all the possibilities. Jesus also speeds up time when He turns water into wine. He gets what normally takes a whole growing season and a lot of work to take place in a few minutes (**John 2:1-12**):

> *On the third day there was a wedding in Cana of Galilee, and the mother of Jesus was there; and both Jesus and His disciples were invited to the wedding. When the wine ran out, the mother of Jesus said to Him, "They have no wine." And Jesus said to her, "Woman, what*

does that have to do with us? My hour has not yet come." His mother said to the servants, "Whatever He says to you, do it." Now there were six stone water pots set there for the Jewish custom of purification, containing twenty or thirty gallons each. Jesus said to them, "Fill the water pots with water." So they filled them up to the brim. And He said to them, "Draw some out now and take it to the headwaiter." So they took it to him. When the headwaiter tasted the water which had become wine, and did not know where it came from (but the servants who had drawn the water knew), the headwaiter called the bridegroom, and said to him, "Every man serves the good wine first, and when the people have drunk freely, then he serves the poorer wine; but you have kept the good wine until now." This beginning of His signs Jesus did in Cana of Galilee, and manifested His glory, and His disciples believed in Him. After this He went down to Capernaum, He and His mother and His brothers and His disciples; and they stayed there a few days.

Another of these time-benders takes place with the men of Keilah and David's request about what they will do. God said King Saul would come down and surround the city and that the men of Keilah would betray David to King Saul. Because of this knowledge, David leaves Keilah. This causes Saul to not come down and the men of Keilah to never be in the position to betray David (**1 Samuel 23:10-14**):

Then David said, "O LORD God of Israel, Your servant has heard for certain that Saul is seeking to come to Keilah to destroy the city on my account. Will the men of Keilah surrender me into his hand? Will Saul come down just as Your servant has heard? O LORD God of Israel, I pray, tell Your servant." And the LORD said, "He will come down." Then David said, "Will the men

> of Keilah surrender me and my men into the hand of Saul?" And the LORD said, "They will surrender you." Then David and his men, about six hundred, arose and departed from Keilah, and they went wherever they could go. When it was told Saul that David had escaped from Keilah, he gave up the pursuit. David stayed in the wilderness in the strongholds, and remained in the hill country in the wilderness of Ziph. And Saul sought him every day, but God did not deliver him into his hand.

This suggests that God told David that if you continue to do what you are currently doing, then this will be the result; but if you choose to do a different thing, then something entirely differently will take place.

When we are ushered into eternity, we are not ushered into the same experience of time but a whole different interaction with time. One enters "the now." There is no past, present, or future but instead just the now. Some people have missed this newness to the time element of eternity and have, therefore, even proposed that heaven would be boring after thousands of years of time. Eternity is "the now."

When Jesus says that the soul of mankind is eternal and life and/or punishment will be eternal. He seems to mean that humans will dwell in this dimension of existence -- either blessed or damned. We cannot even fully comprehend what that is like.

Eternity is like flying up into time as though time is a substance like air or water. If we could experience this right now in this world, we could theoretically explore everything that was happening in any one minute of the world's existence without moving on to the next moment in linear time. In other words, I could experience what my sister is currently experiencing, what my wife is experiencing, what my children are going through, and what my boss is living through all without moving forward in linear time.

BECAUSE OUR SOULS ARE IMMORTAL.

The reality of hell was for centuries one of the controlling impulses for the preaching of the good news of Christ. People have an eternal soul that they need to take care of and orient it towards righteousness through repentance and faith or they will be swallowed by eternity and spend eternity condemned when they could have been pardoned.

When the truth of hell and its inescapability hits our consciousness, we usually become much more urgent in our appeals to others about repenting and seeking God's forgiveness. Eventually we settle into being more sensitive for any opportunity to share with people their peril and their need for the Savior.

3. Hell exists because people's choices are real.

Hell exists because choices matter. God in His Sovereignty gives us real choices and they have eternal consequences (Romans 3:10-18; Matthew 22:37-40; John 3:16). God is looking for lovers and worshippers to populate eternity (John 4:24). The power of choice must be honored or love is not possible.

Listen in as Lee Strobel and J.P. Moreland have an agitated exchange about the reality of people's choices:

"You are saying that people consciously choose Hell?"

"No, I don't mean they consciously reject heaven and choose to go to hell instead. But they do choose not to care about the kinds of values that will be present in heaven every day. So, in effect, by the way we live our lives we're either preparing ourselves for being in God's presence and enjoying him for eternity or we're preparing ourselves for an existence where we try to make ourselves the center of the universe and we have no interest in being with God or the people who love Him."5

Hell is a monument to the choices of mankind (and angels); even the choice to reject God and worship that which is not God. There is a need for choice to be more than illusion. Choice must be more than secondary causes of a cosmic primary cause. If our choices don't mean anything but are really some pre-planned play scripted by the Creator, then He is the author of evil and anyone's assignment to hell is nonsensical and even wicked. But God tells us that it is our deeds, our choices, and our words that will be our judges (Romans 2:5-7). Our choices do matter and whether we rebel or embrace God's righteousness has huge consequences.

> **Romans 2:5-7** - *But because of your stubbornness and unrepentant heart you are storing up wrath for yourself in the day of wrath and revelation of the righteous judgment of God, who WILL RENDER TO EACH PERSON ACCORDING TO HIS DEEDS: to those who by perseverance in doing good seek for glory and honor and immortality, eternal life.*

Choice is real and not a figment of our imagination. Right now counts forever. Make choices that move you into and along the path of righteousness. Look at what Jesus says to the people of Jerusalem about their choices:

> **Luke 13:34,35** - *O Jerusalem, Jerusalem, the city that kills the prophets and stones those sent to her! How often I wanted to gather your children together, just as a hen gathers her brood under her wings, <u>and you would not</u>*

have it! *Behold, your house is left to you desolate; and I say to you, you will not see Me until the time comes when you say, "BLESSED IS HE WHO COMES IN THE NAME OF THE LORD"*

Their choices were real and the fact that they made bad ones means that the wrong consequences flowed into their lives

There are only a few real Christian answers as to why the world exists. The dominant Christian theological view on why God created the universe is based upon John 4:24-26. God is searching for worshippers who will worship Him in Spirit and in truth. Christians have always believed that God created the world to draw out, over the centuries, a multitude of people who really love Him, want to worship Him, and be drawn into the wonder of His joy and life.

John 4:22-27 - *You worship what you do not know; we worship what we know, for salvation is from the Jews. But an hour is coming, and now is, when the true worshipers will worship the Father in spirit and truth; for such people the Father seeks to be His worshipers. God is spirit, and those who worship Him must worship in spirit and truth. The woman said to Him, "I know that Messiah is coming (He who is called Christ); when that One comes, He will declare all things to us." Jesus said to her, "I who speak to you am He." At this point His disciples came, and they were amazed that He had been speaking with a woman, yet no one said, "What do You seek?" or "Why do You speak with her?"*

These verses state that God wanted to create creatures that could enjoy the wonder of His presence and life. He therefore created creatures who could really choose to love Him and/or could really choose to reject Him. For it is not possible to have real love without real choice. He knew that they would choose poorly and doom the whole human race to death and destruction. He instituted a redemption system to give people the opportunity to accomplish His original goal through His plan and His work.

In order to have an authentic plan for this to happen, God must give humanity real choices with real consequences. Real love requires real choices. God must give people the right to truly reject Him. God did what was required to find real worshippers -- people who would really love Him. He gave them real choices. This way of finding true worshippers is messy and uneven. In order to deal with the sin, damage, and destruction of allowing humans the power of real choice, God sent His only begotten Son here to live a perfect life, voluntarily die for the sins of the whole world and, thereby, to affect a rescue of those who wanted to enjoy the presence and joy of God. Left to ourselves we would make the wrong choice again so God sent His Holy Spirit to give people the ability to choose and to draw people to the Savior. In this way God draws many to Himself and He can give them eternal life. Many still choose to reject the Savior and His invitation, but it was their choice.

This is a crucial part of the Christian message. This is not a popular element of the Christian message but it is a part of the message. There is a heaven to gain and a hell to lose. God did not have to provide the remedy that would take care of our soiled condition, but He did out of love for us. Christ's appearance is evidence of God's love.

> You have to understand that people's character is nor formed by decisions all at once, but by thousands of little choices they make every day without even knowing about it. Each day we're preparing ourselves for either being with God and his people and valuing the things He values, or

choosing not to engage with those things. So yes Hell is primarily a place for people who would not want to go to heaven.[6]

Some have suggested that since God is love, He will redeem everyone; and they will all become submissive believers in God. This is called Universalism. The problem with Universalism is that in order for this to be true, God must force many people to accept a salvation that they do not want. They do not want to relinquish the control of their life. They cling to their own deity. God respects their choice and it continues to be their choice -- a choice that they do not repent of and eventually are unable to repent of it.

Because choices, actions, and words create real causal events that ripple on forever.

This is not a paper-mache world where we are only puppets on a cosmic stage, speaking lines that change nothing. Our choices, actions, and words have value and solidity. God told Adam and Eve that they had permanently changed the world by their rebellious and selfish choice (Genesis 3:11-24). Choices, decisions, and words change the course of events. They echo into eternity. As one popular theologian is fond of saying, **"Right now counts forever."**

Remember, because choices count forever, we should beg people to repent and go a different way than continue indulging their own selfishness. Remind yourself of how important Jesus saw our choices, our words, and our actions.

Why Does There Have To Be A Hell - Part 1

John 3:16 - *For God so loved the world, that He gave His only begotten Son, that whoever <u>believes</u> in Him shall not perish, but have eternal life.*

Our choices to embrace the forgiveness that is in Christ can set us free from the wrath of God that will land upon us. Our choices can literally set us free. Every righteous choice leads to more righteous and blessed choices. Every selfish, unrighteous choice leads to more selfish, unrighteous choices. This choice multiplier very quickly can move us to places that we would not recognize from where we stand presently.

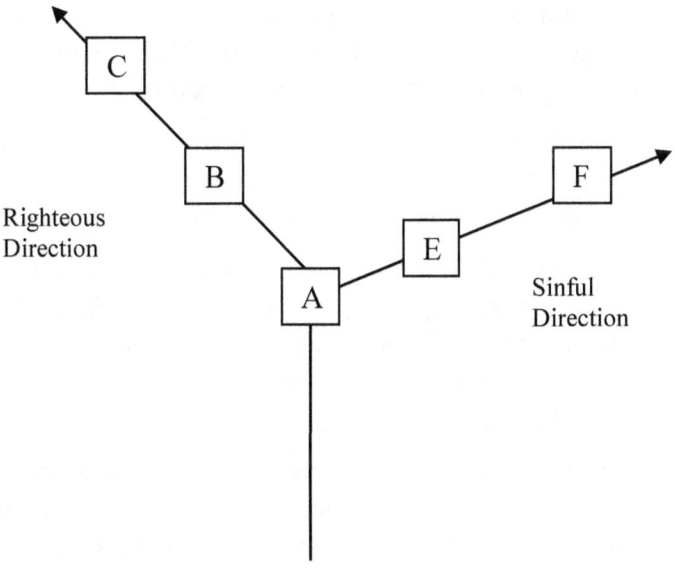

A person comes to decision point A and can go to the left toward decisions B and C which is the righteous direction, or this person can go toward decisions E and F which is the sinful direction. Look at the diagram to see how the choice multiplier radically changes the options in only two decisions. If a person makes two righteous decisions that are a long way from the same person making two sinful decisions, it doesn't take very long for a person's path in life to get very different with righteous or sinful choices.

> **Matthew 12:36,37** - *But I tell you that every careless word that people speak, they shall give an accounting for it in the day of judgment. For by your words you will be justified, and by your words you will be condemned.*

Jesus tells us that for every word we speak, we will give an accounting for. This level of judgment is unheard of in western culture, but it is what Jesus says will happen on judgment day. Have you ever said things that have damaged or even destroyed others? Have people said things to you that you have never forgotten?

> **Matthew 5:21,22** - *You have heard that the ancients were told, "YOU SHALL NOT COMMIT MURDER" and "Whoever commits murder shall be liable to the court."*
>
> *But I say to you that everyone who is angry with his brother shall be guilty before the court; and whoever says to his brother, "You good-for-nothing," shall be guilty before the supreme court; and whoever says, "You fool," shall be guilty enough to go into the fiery hell.*

It is clear from this verse that actions and even emotional outbursts will be evaluated for their benefit or harm to others. We are responsible for what we say, do, think, and emote. Even though our culture thinks that we cannot expect people to control themselves in these areas, this is not what God declares.

> **John 3:36** - *He who believes in the Son has eternal life; but he who does not obey the Son will not see life, but the wrath of God abides on him.*

Why Does There Have To Be A Hell - Part 1

One of the joys of the Christian message is that at any time in our lives -- even though we are way down the wrong road -- we can repent from our ways and head out towards the country of righteousness, and God will walk with us and get us there. Yes, we will have missed many blessings we could have had, but we will immediately begin receiving the blessings and mercy of the righteous direction. We will also have new righteous choices appear to us.

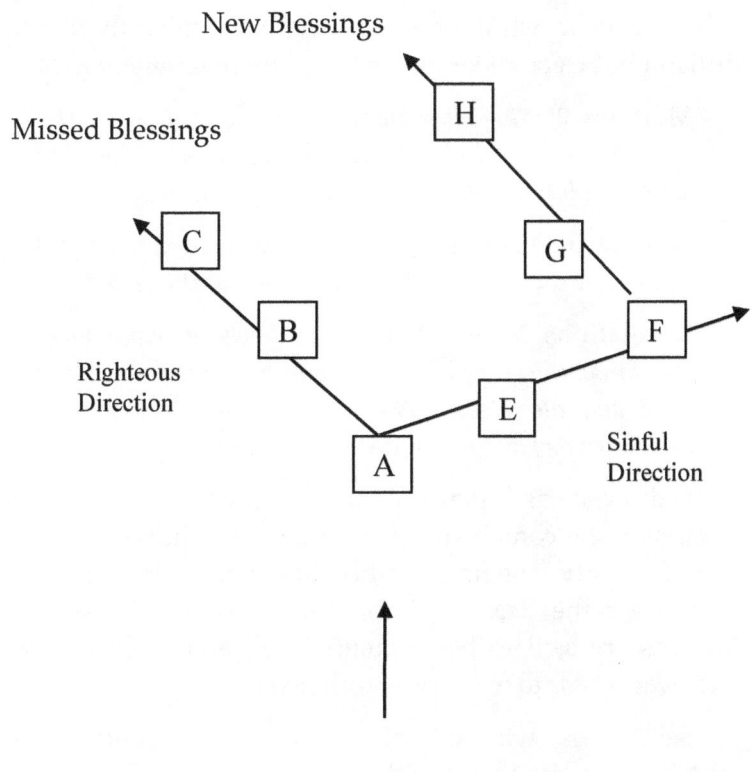

4. **Hell exists because God needed a containment field for the eternal souls of angels and humans who would defy His love and would chose to go their own self-centered, independent way.**

Why would God build hell and the lake of fire? We have an implicit desire that God would just cause people to cease to exist. But the soul is eternal for both angels and humans. He also declares that He values their worth too greatly to just abolish their lives and their choices. Therefore hell and the lake of fire are containment vessels. Notice the restricted movement in and out. The toxicity of sin and rebellion must be contained, so God builds a prison from which there is no escape. Examine these two difficult but clear verses regarding this containment field:

Matthew 25:41 - *Then He will also say to those on His left, 'Depart from Me, accursed ones, into the eternal fire which has been prepared for the devil and his angels'*

Look at Revelation 20:10 and how God describes the end for the Antichrist, the False Prophet, and the Devil.

Revelations 20:10 - *And the devil who deceived them was thrown into the lake of fire and brimstone, where the beast and the false prophet are also; and they will be tormented day and night forever and ever.*

Hell exists as a place for the Devil and his corrupted demons to be contained, quarantined, and judged for the rest of eternity. The first two human inhabitants of the lake of fire are the Beast and the False Prophet. These two humans are said to be tormented day and night forever and ever -- or into eternity -- with no escape.

Selfishness, wickedness, and sin would contaminate eternity as it has this world if it were allowed. These evil traits will continue to live in the angelic and human individuals who have become corrupted during their life.

Those who defy His love and chose to go their own independent way must be contained so that the toxicity of sin will not spread in eternity as it has in this world.

God's wrath is the righteous expression of His displeasure at the persistent selfishness and rebelliousness of humankind. All their thoughts are corrupt (**Romans 3:10-18**):

> *As it is written, There is none righteous, not even one; There is none who understand, There is none who seeks for God; All have turned aside, Together they have become useless; There is none who does good, There is not even one. Their throat is an open grave, with their tongues they keep deceiving, The poison of asps is under their lips; Whose mouth is full of cursing and bitterness; Their feet are swift to shed blood, Destruction and misery are in their paths, And the path of peace they have not known. There is no fear of God before their eyes."*

They will never think of the greater good but only how any and every action affects them or benefits them

Selfishness, wickedness, and rebellion grow -- even as we have seen in this world -- unless it is supernaturally contained. What is interesting about the Scriptural account of this containment is that there is no mention of the annihilation of the Devil, only of his defeat. One would think that he would be completely eliminated through nonexistence. However, he is an eternal being that has gone wrong and therefore must serve an eternal containment.

Listen to J.P. Moreland, again, in his insightful comment about the nature and significance of hell:

> Remember that hell will forever be a monument to human dignity and the value of human choice. It is a quarantine where God says two important things. "I respect freedom of choice enough to where I won't coerce people, and I value my image-bearers so much that I will not annihilate them.⁷

5. Hell exists because selfishness grows even after death.

Hell exists because selfishness grows even after death and will eventually twist everyone into something abhorrent and disgusting. As we saw with the rich man who was in Hades, he remained selfish, haughty, oppressive, and self-righteous toward Abraham and the poor man, Lazarus. Remember the principle **"WHAT YOU ARE IN THIS LIFE, YOU BECOME MORE OF IN THE AFTERLIFE."** We should come to Christ to be set free from the principle of sin that lives within us so that we don't have to spend eternity in a God-constructed warehouse to contain our growing selfishness. There is no repentance from the path of unrighteousness in hell so it just grows and grows.

> *Luke 16:24, 27, 30 - And he cried out and said, "Father Abraham, have mercy on me, and send Lazarus so that he may dip the tip of his finger in water and cool off my tongue, for I am in agony in this flame." And he said, "Then I beg you, father, that you send him to my father's house -- But he said, "No, father Abraham, but if someone goes to them from the dead, they will repent!"*

Notice the haughtiness and the condescending tone the rich man has towards Lazarus and even Abraham. Does the rich man sound like he has seen the error of his ways?

Look at what comes out of the bottomless pit in Revelation 9. These fallen angels that have been contained since the time of Noah do not emerge from their confinement in a part of hell with a repentant heart and a submissive spirit. No, they are more bent on the destruction of mankind than when they went in.

Because we only see seventy or eighty years of an individual's selfish development -- which is often contained and hidden by cultural, family, and societal norms -- we are often fooled into believing that people are not that bad.

D.A. Carson, the New Testament scholar, grasps the idea of hell's inhabitants quite clearly in an interview with Lee Strobel:

> Hell is not a place where people are consigned because they were pretty good blokes, but they just didn't believe the right stuff. They're consigned there, first and foremost, because they defy their maker and want to be at the center of the universe. Hell is not filled with people who have already repented, only God isn't gentle enough or good enough to let them out. It's filled with people who, for all eternity, still want to be the center of the universe and who persist in their God-defying rebellion.[8]

Look again at Revelation 22:15. Notice the present tense verbs and continuing practices of evil. Even when the people are confined to the lake of fire their practices of lying, immorality, murder and idolatry continue. Selfishness continues to grow even in the lake of fire.

They are still lying; the practice continues. The corruption of their soul is continuing.

Why There Has To Be A Hell

Revelation 22:15 - *Outside are the dogs and the sorcerers and the immoral persons and the murderers and the idolaters, and everyone who loves and practices lying.*

Chapter 5

Part II

Why Does There Have To Be A Hell?

6. Hell exists because of the butterfly effects of sin.

The butterfly effect is the connectedness of all things and the cascading results of small changes. This idea has not been explored sufficiently in terms of the consequences of sin. Scientists are regularly proclaiming the butterfly effect in terms of the connectedness of all things in our world. If a butterfly flaps its wings in Africa, it may develop a hurricane off the coast of the United States.

Each and every sin a person commits is a choice, an action, a spoken word that ripples out from them and creates a cascade of effects throughout their lives, their family, their community, and potentially the world. Our culture tries to suppress this continuing impact of sin because a true understanding of what happens each time a person chooses sin over righteousness would stop the sensuality and greed of our culture. If we were to really understand what the destruction that flows from one decision to cheat on your spouse, one decision to steal from our company, one decision to curse out a colleague, one decision to deceive your boss, we would pull back. But the impact of our selfishness, rebellion, and sinfulness is undeniable. God is not deceived about the continuing and cascading impact of sin through the world, and He has built a containment field called hell and eventually the lake of fire.

Let's take a look at just one example of which we could multiply thousands of times in different arenas. We know that our Western culture, as well as the world, is seeing a resurgence of human trafficking for sex. People are being bought and sold as slaves. This proliferation of this modern slave trade can clearly be traced to the tolerance of adultery in the west and amongst the peoples of the world. Our culture has adopted a very casual attitude to adultery in all of its forms. Our culture asks the question:

> What does it hurt that a man or a woman is unfaithful to their spouse?

> What harm does it cause if a man or woman has sexual relations with someone they are not married to?

> All of this past worry about sexual abstinence and sexual faithfulness are just the antiquated values of a bygone era.

> We don't need that now.

But it is the appetite for non-committal and no-consequences sex that brings the increasing demand that ultimately develops into human trafficking for sex. It is easy to overlook the adultery all around us because we do not see the storms that these actions produce around the world. But God sees it all. If we were to actually see all the consequences of our sins and wicked actions as it ripples out through our families, communities, and across generations, we would have ample evidence for the need for hell and justice. We are so naïve about sin. It is possible that someday in eternity we will see how each of our actions has contributed to not only our own destruction and/or lack of success but also to our families and others in our country and those in the future.

Proverbs 21:15 - *The exercise of justice is joy for the righteous, but is terror to the workers of iniquity.*

The only way that the exercise of justice is joy is when we see the harm that we are containing, preventing, recovering, and/or condemning. It is our limited perspective on the impact of sin that allows us to put up with the sin and wickedness that we do.

Let me tell you two stories to hopefully bring this idea home. There was a man in a church who, through his association with the pastor, was trusted to deposit the offering money each week. At some point he decided that he could begin embezzling funds from the church before it was deposited. He got away with this for over a dozen years. His extra money allowed his family to live well above their means. His children grew up with the idea that money was the highest value. Later this man's daughter grew up and became involved in a murder-for-inheritance plot that caused the death of one man and led to the suicide of his wife. Certain officials stated that there was strong connection between the daughter's willingness to stay with the plot until a murder had been committed because of watching the father stay with the embezzling for so many years from the church. The butterfly effect of the father's sin is rippling out in ways he never imagined.

Let me give you another true story. A young father began molesting his oldest daughter and the mother took the child and left. The father was not confronted nor was the sin exposed. The man remarried a young woman with children and the man began, after a short period of time, to molest these new "daughters." This new mother -- rather than leave -- began to defend the father and cover up the father's sin. More children were born and the molestation continued. Eventually the father died an early death and the children have needed years of counseling and work to process what was allowed to happen to them. None of them seem to show the drive to fulfill the talent and abilities that they possess. The mother when she needed help in her older years was largely abandoned by the children. They also want to have little to nothing to do with their mother who allowed this abuse to take place. Few who knew them could explain the hostility between the mother and the children because they did not know the back story. The sinful decision of this man and this woman will have echoing effects through the generations. The likelihood of dysfunction and devastation being continued in at least one of the families is high. It is so tragic. Sin grows and keeps destroying.

Each and every sin brings not just individual consequences but familial consequences, community consequences, and societal consequences as well as future consequences. Sin and wickedness create consequences that echo across communities and families and also down through the centuries. One of the classic ways to see this on a limited scale is to do a genogram of your own family and trace the significant events, traumas, and sinful actions in your family. It becomes readily apparent how the sin of one parent ripples through generations and changes the future for families.

Just look at the genogram of Abraham's family.

Abraham lies about Sarah his wife twice in order to save his own skin. Then Isaac lies about his wife Rebekah. Then Jacob becomes a liar, cheat, and swindler in order to gain what he wants. Sin is not isolated, but it grows through individuals and families. It can be stopped but only through the grace of God injected into an individual's life.

It involves not just what we do but what we are not doing. It is the bad road taken and all of its consequences but also the good road not taken and all of the blessings and joys not experienced on that road. It may be the blessings and glories of that road that were needed for you and your family to maximize their joy. But you did not take that road.

Hell is an awful place of containment because sin is awful in its impact and continuing effects. We are so limited in our understanding of this. And our culture helps to hide the power of sin because it wants to encourage us to participate in it (Romans 1:28-32).

Because we are only able to be informed about a limited amount of the impact of one sin, we do not see its spreading contagion; and so we excuse our actions as inconsequential. Every time there is an outbreak of a pandemic, there are a few individuals who are carriers of the disease and refuse to believe that their "innocent" actions could cause all this uproar.

We are unaware of the endless impact of each of our selfish and sinful actions. One act of selfishness can produce a rape, murder, or corruption of government in another part of the world or in a succeeding generation. As we study this more and more it becomes clear that even though we do not understand all the reasons and rationale, there is a need for hell.

When I ask people if they have sinned, most will say "yes." When I ask what they think the consequences of those sins are, they will usually talk only about negative consequences to themselves. They will rarely bring up negative consequences to others. I have never had a person bring up long-term dysfunction that has or will potentially spring up because of their sinful choices or actions. We just do not understand the awfulness of sin. But God does and that is why there is a hell.

7. HELL EXISTS BECAUSE GOD IS OMNISCIENT AND UNCHANGING.

In the western world we are being told that ethics are nothing more than our individual emotional reactions to events. Therefore, according to this theory of ethics what is today repulsive and therefore wrong could in a few years be normal and therefore acceptable. This is how we have moved into a culture where lying, stealing, and adultery are accepted as normal and then protected by civil laws.

God, however, did not build the moral structure of the universe based upon an emotional reaction to events or actions nor through votes in heaven or in the ideas of a particular local culture. He built the moral structure of the world out of the rightness of His attributes and the perfections of His nature. The essence of ethics is what will cause benefits and do no harm to the individual, the family, and/or the community. God does know what is best for these beings that He created. He has given us both externally and internally the basic rules which will create a healthy individual, a healthy family network, and a healthy community (Romans 2:15). We call these the moral law or the Ten Commandments. These outline the universal moral law for mankind. What God said was sin millennia ago is still sin. What God says will wreck a nation or community will wreck a group of people in the modern day. He has not changed His mind; therefore there is a hell.

Listen to Lee Strobel's discussion with J.P. Moreland on the nature of God and hell:

> If God is just a child with arbitrary rules, then it would be capricious for him to sentence people.
>
> God is the most generous, loving, wonderful, attractive being in the cosmos. He has made us with free will and he has made us for a purpose; to relate loving to Him, and to others. We are not accidents, we are not modified monkeys, we are not random mistakes. And if we fail over and over again to live for the purpose for which we were made – a purpose, by the way, which would allow us to flourish more than living any other way, then God will have absolutely no choice but to give us what we've asked for all along in our lives, which is separation from him. And that is hell.[1]

We usually perceive whether something makes sense as much emotionally as we do rationally. There are some truths that are so difficult to deal with that we block them out of our minds to deal with later or we deny that they are happening or will happen. Bernie Madoff, the disgraced financier, said that he knew as soon as he started his giant ponzi scheme that one day the FBI, NYPD, and/or SEC would come and arrest him. But yet he kept living in denial and kept swindling people out of millions of dollars of their life savings. He kept living in luxury as though nothing was wrong.

There are a great many things that are happening in our society and in our lives every day that we choose to just not think about. This emotional factor is what clouds our ability to see reality at times. The truth just doesn't feel right to us. We cry out, "How can that be?"

There are many examples down through history of an inability to accept truth emotionally, so it is ignored. The germ theory of disease was ignored and patients kept getting sick and dying because doctors would not wash their hands between patients. Many could not emotionally embrace the general theory of relativity, so they refused to accept its truth. Many find it difficult, if not impossible, to accept the truth about adultery in all of its forms because they enjoy committing it and have allowed their practice of it to define them.

In the same way, many cannot envision a world in which consequences count forever. They cannot envision a need for a place where those who continually expressed a selfish, corrupting, immoral tendency would need to exist so that they do not contaminate the larger space with their ideas and tendencies. There is still too much materialism and naturalism in modern understanding of death and the afterlife. Many people want hell to have an end so that their concept of suffering and punishment is upheld. They cannot understand why God would not just wipe out of existence those whose choices have brought them to a self-perpetuating corruption that cannot be stopped but only contained. They are uncomfortable with a system that actually takes people's choices seriously. They are unwilling to think through the idea that one's choices build a rut that they will most likely stay in for the remainder of their lives. This rut is confirmed at the transition through the doorway called death. A person becomes more and more of what they already are.

8. HELL EXISTS BECAUSE THE HIERARCHICAL ORDER OF BEING.

Any offense against the Supreme Being is more heinous than offenses against a lesser being. This argument about the innate worthiness of God is lost on people who do not believe in God, angels, or humanity as a special creation of God; but the hierarchy of being exists.

In our culture we remain significantly naïve of the difference between God and the other forms of life that populate the planet. We intrinsically understand that some forms of life are more valuable than others; but few have thought about the impact of offending the Supreme Being because we are so myopically focused on our own wounds, hurts, and offenses.

If you created a world in which every delight and satisfying experience were potentially provided, how would you feel if the creatures that you gave these treasures to turned against you and instead decided to defy you and demand their freedom from your blessings and grace? You would feel, in a small way, what God feels -- saddened, amazed, grieved, and angry at the rebellion, stupidity, and foolishness you were seeing.

Jesus suggests a reason for the existence of hell that was explored much more thoroughly in the Middle Ages than in our modern world. This line of reasoning has been called the argument from the hierarchical order of being. Notice what Jesus says in **Matthew 6:25-30**:

> For this reason I say to you, do not be worried about your life, as to what you will eat or what you will drink; nor for your body, as to what you will put on. Is not life more than food, and the body more than clothing? Look at the birds of the air, that they do not sow, nor reap nor gather into barns, and yet your heavenly Father feeds them. <u>Are you not worth much more than they?</u> And

who of you by being worried can add a single hour to his life? "And why are you worried about clothing? Observe how the lilies of the field grow; they do not toil nor do they spin, yet I say to you that not even Solomon in all his glory clothed himself like one of these. But if God so clothes the grass of the field, which is alive today and tomorrow is thrown into the furnace, will He not much more clothe you? You of little faith!

The argument for hell from the hierarchical order of being goes something like this: Most people recognize that plant life is living but less valuable than animal life and that bacterial life and insect life also falls along a line of importance. There is some life that is more valuable than others. Jesus says this when He values human life more than the birds of the field and when he values the grass of the field less than Solomon. It is important at this point to state that all human life is created equal in value. Humanity has consistently run into trouble by trying to apply this idea within the human species.

If it is true that there are forms of life that are more valuable than others, then it follows that God, who is the highest being, is more offended by words of rebellion than murdering blades of grass. When I was a little boy I mercilessly used a magnifying glass to burn ants in the hot sun and yet I was not arrested. I was, on the other hand, severely reprimanded by my parents for speaking words of disrespect to adults. We see in this typical parental behavior a distinction in value between certain living species on this planet and others. There is an almost inherent, increasing value that ascends with the increasing complexity of the species.

We make laws that protect humans from violence, slander, kidnapping, oppression, rape, and even stealing. But we do not prosecute the beekeeper for stealing the product of the bees. We do not prosecute the pig farmer for murdering the pig in order to provide food and sell at a profit. We do not prosecute kennels for kidnapping dogs from their litter and giving them away to families permanently. We have the laws that we have because we innately understand the hierarchical order of being. Yes, some of our laws need to be reexamined so that we are not cruel or inhumane to animals. But seeing that we value humanity above animals, reptiles, insects, and plant life, we should realize that God is the highest value. Any offense committed against God is an offence of the highest order. Our culture has little appreciation for offenses against the spirit world and against God. We have dismantled the idea of the sacred and applaud those who move along this line no matter how degrading this debunking of the sacred becomes. In fact, we seem to revel in our debunking and reviling of spiritual realities. But our offenses against God are real. He is our creator and sustainer and our rebellion and disrespect in the face of His clear testimony and love is an offense of the highest order.

9. HELL EXISTS BECAUSE OF THE EXISTENCE OF A POINT OF NO RETURN IN EVERY PERSON'S LIFE. HEBREWS 9:27; HEBREWS 6:4-8; MATTHEW 11:20-24; MATTHEW 12:30-32; MATTHEW 23:33.

Even though our culture is at war with God, it has integrated the grace of God and repentance into its thinking. We love the second chance. We demand the right to change our mind. We believe that people can change. These are all functions of the grace of God. God allows U-turns in life. He continues to call people to repentance (to change one's mind) and to start moving in step with Him. This idea of grace, mercy, and repentance has been looked on as a right that extends as long as a person is conscious. God is radically gracious, but He says that there will come a time when you reach the point of no return in terms of repentance. For some that point is the moments before death; for others it is in their middle-twenties. God is under no obligation to allow people to continue living after they have reached the point of no return.

Hell exists because everyone comes to a point of no return or permanence (fixity) in regards to their relationship with righteousness; they are either for it or against it -- permanently. Another way of saying this is that there is a point in everyone's life where their orientation toward righteousness becomes fixed and there is no going back from that point. There is no repentance past this point; one's orientation only grows and progresses in the same direction after this point.

> If all a person needed was a little bit more time to come to Christ, then God would extend their time on this earth to give them that chance. So there will be nobody who just needed a little more time or who died prematurely who would have responded to another chance to receive Christ.[2]

The wonderful thing about the Christian gospel is that many who we have thought were past this point of no return have changed their mind and opened themselves to the grace of God. I remember one lady who was in the community where I was starting a new church. She was employed by the school where our little fledgling church was meeting. She did everything she could to close down the church or to get us kicked off school grounds. She hid our sound system. She moved our piano out into the rain after we were promised it would be safe. She convinced teachers to not let us use their classrooms for Sunday School rooms. She took it upon herself to bad mouth us to everyone at the school. If there was one person who I thought was permanently closed to the gospel, it was this lady. But about ten years later I bumped into this woman. She approached me somewhat sheepishly. She asked me if I remembered her. I told that I did remember her, and I asked how her husband and family were doing. She said that she needed to apologize for how she had treated the church I was leading. After she had moved away she accidently ended up going to a church near her new house. She listened to the message and over a period of a month she became a Christian. She knew that she would eventually need to have a conversation with me about all that she had done to destroy the church, and she was hoping I would forgive her. Of course I forgave her and was excited about her new found faith in Christ.

Let's look at these Scriptures that speak of this point of fixity.

> **Hebrews 9:27** - *And inasmuch as it is appointed for men to die once and after this comes judgment*

Death is definitely a point of fixity, but some people reach their point of fixity before death as we shall see. There is no repentance after that point. For most humans it is at the point of death. For some it is well before their physical death. For angels it was when they chose to join Satan's rebellion or continue in loyal worship and love of God Almighty.

What we are in life is confirmed in death and eternity! We become more of what we already were. We may protest our place, but it will be from the perspective we developed in this life. C.S. Lewis said that a small error in foundation is not bad in a one-story building. But it is catastrophic in a 100-story skyscraper.

> Remember, if God really does let people shape their own character by the thousands of choices they make, he is also going to allow them to suffer the

natural consequences of that character that they have chosen to have.[3]

Every human -- the Bible declares -- since Adam and Eve have had a bent towards unrighteousness and evil (Romans 3:23; 5:12). This original sin which is active within them eventually moves them to commit acts of unrighteousness (Romans 3:10-18). But humans, during their lifetime, have the opportunity to turn around (repent) from this natural inclination toward selfish unrighteousness. This is called repentance and is offered by the grace of God through the life, death, and resurrection of Jesus the Christ.

Angelic beings were offered the choice to continue worshipping and following God or to participate in the rebellion of Lucifer (Revelation 12:3,4,7-9; Isaiah 14:12-16; Ezekiel 28:11-18). Their choice sealed their fate permanently. There is no repentance for them. Their point of fixity was that choice.

> **Hebrews 6:4-8** - *For in the case of those who have once been enlightened and have tasted of the heavenly gift and have been made partakers of the Holy Spirit, and have tasted the good word of God and the powers of the age to come, and then have fallen away, it is impossible to renew them again to repentance, since they again crucify to themselves the Son of God and put Him to open shame. For ground that drinks the rain which often falls on it and brings forth vegetation useful to those for whose sake it is also tilled, receives a blessing from God; but if it yields thorns and thistles, it is worthless and close to being cursed, and it ends up being burned.*

This verse is a controversial passage but whoever these ideas apply to, it is clear that at some point during their earthly life before death they have reached a point of fixity in relationship to righteousness. This person became unredeemable even though this person was still alive. This verse makes it clear that the point of fixity is not always death.

> **Matthew 11:20-24** - *Then He began to denounce the cities in which most of His miracles were done, because they did not repent. "Woe to you, Chorazin! Woe to you, Bethsaida! For if the miracles had occurred in Tyre and Sidon which occurred in you, they would have repented long ago in sackcloth and ashes. Nevertheless I say to you, <u>it will be more tolerable for Tyre and Sidon in the day of judgment than for you.</u> And you, Capernaum, will not be exalted to heaven, will you? You will descend to Hades; for if the miracles had occurred in Sodom which occurred in you, it would have remained to this day. Nevertheless I say to you that <u>it will be more tolerable for the land of Sodom in the day of judgment, than for you.</u>"*

These three cities on the northern coast of the Sea of Galilee, which were blessed to have the Son of God set up shop in their cities, missed their appointed time. The city leaders had reached their point of fixity most likely because they had ignored all the miracles and teaching of Jesus. They were at this point fixed in their orientation to Jesus and righteousness. They were selfish, sinful, and resistant to the things of God. They were headed to hell.

> **Matthew 12:30-32** - *He who is not with Me is against Me; and he who does not gather with Me scatters. Therefore I say to you, any sin and blasphemy shall be forgiven people, but blasphemy against the Spirit shall not be forgiven. Whoever speaks a word against the Son of Man, it shall be forgiven him; <u>but whoever speaks against the Holy Spirit, it shall not be forgiven him, either in this age or in the age to come.</u>*

The point of fixity in this passage is the blasphemy against the Holy Spirit. Theologians disagree as to how this sin is committed but when it is committed, it causes a person to cross a line of fixity from which there is no turning back. It is possible for people to so resist the ministry of the Holy Spirit in their lives that they become hardened in that condition permanently.

Matthew 23:33 - *You serpents, you brood of vipers, how will you escape the sentence of hell?*

By the time Jesus utters His warnings in Matthew 24, He had reached His limit with these self-proclaimed religious bigots, so He tells them that they had already punched their tickets for hell. They had become fixed in relation to God and true righteousness. They were against it because true righteousness would dismantle their system. There was no turning back for many of these officials.

Look at Milton's comments in *Paradise Lost* about the mental state of the Devil and the fixity of perspective in hell. We see the Devil proclaim the following:

> Hail, horrors, hail
>
> infernal world, and thou profoundest Hell.
>
> Receive thy new possessor; One who brings
>
> a mind not to be changed by place and time.
>
> The mind is its own place and in itself
>
> Can make a Heaven of Hell, and a Hell of Heaven.[4]

Jesus hints at the reality of a place in each of our existences where we reach a place of fixity. We keep becoming more of what we were at that point.

10. Hell exists because the inspired authorities on the afterlife say it exists and will exist forever: Jesus, The Apostles, and The Scriptures as a whole.

The overwhelming testimony of Scripture shouts to us that hell is real, and we must prepare ourselves and help others prepare for escaping this reality. We have been commissioned with a message from God: Hell is eternal and is waiting for all those who are sinful, selfish, and wicked. Cry out for God's mercy. Flee into the arms of Jesus who offers the only hope of mercy and grace.

Let's look at some other verses we have not examined where Jesus comments on hell:

> **Mark 9:42-49** - *Whoever causes one of these little ones who believe to stumble, it would be better for him if, with a heavy millstone hung around his neck, he had been cast into the sea. If your hand causes you to stumble, cut it off; it is better for you to enter life crippled, than, having your two hands, to go into hell, <u>into the unquenchable fire</u>, [where THEIR WORM DOES NOT DIE, AND THE FIRE IS NOT QUENCHED.] If your foot causes you to stumble, cut it off; it is better for you to enter life lame, than, having your two feet, <u>to be cast into hell</u>, [where THEIR WORM DOES NOT DIE, AND THE FIRE IS NOT QUENCHED.] If your eye causes you to stumble, throw it out; it is better for you to enter the kingdom of God with one eye, than, having two eyes, <u>to be cast into hell, where THEIR WORM DOES NOT DIE, AND THE FIRE IS NOT QUENCHED.</u> For everyone will be salted with fire.*

It is clear that Jesus wants His hearers to understand the horrors of hell. They should avoid hell at all costs. Jesus describes the conditions of hell: the worm does not die and there is unquenchable fire. Whatever the fire is, it is unquenchable. It does not let up; it continues to consume. We saw this same kind of fire in Luke 16:19-26, and it did not function like earthly fire. The rich man who was in this unquenchable fire could talk, move, argue, plan, and do a number of other things that people cannot do if they are in earthly fire. The key ingredient in this kind of fire, Jesus tells us, is that it is unquenchable; it cannot be put out. The worm that doesn't die is another evocative image that hell is eternal. There is no end to the consumption that goes on in that place. This is a picture of a place where the breakdown of the person does not stop.

Matthew 8:12 - *But the sons of the kingdom will be cast out into the outer darkness; in that place there will be weeping and gnashing of teeth.*

Jesus emphasizes with this statement about hell being the outer darkness that these people who are excluded from the kingdom of God are outside of where the life and joy happens. They are in the dark. They are excluded. People will be weeping that they are excluded, and they will be gnashing their teeth that they are excluded. It is entirely possible that the gnashing of the teeth involves anger and venting at God who would exclude them.

Matthew 23:33 - *You serpents, you brood of vipers, how will you escape the sentence of hell?*

Jesus does not shy away from saying that some people will be sentenced to hell. And in this case it was not just the expected people but the religious leaders who Jesus calls out for their wicked ways. They hid the truth of God and oppressed honest seekers would be sentenced to hell. This was shocking for Him to say it. Yet it was true. Hell opens up its mouth to swallow those who have pursued a path of wickedness instead of love. It consumes those who have promoted selfish, rebellious actions instead of humbling, embracing through faith the sacrifice of Christ in our place as the only acceptable sacrifice for our sins.

Matthew 10:28 - *Do not fear those who kill the body but are unable to kill the soul; but rather <u>fear Him who is able to destroy both soul and body in hell</u>.*

Some have used the word *destroy* to suggest that God will ultimately disintegrate the people in hell. But clearly other passages state that this destruction continues without interruption: the worm does not die, unquenchable fire, everlasting contempt, eternal torment, eternal punishment night and day forever and ever. In other words, whatever this consumptive destructive process is, it does not end.

Finally, I don't believe in reincarnation because there's an expert on this question, and he's Jesus of Nazareth. He's the only person in history who died, rose from the dead, and spoke authoritatively on the question. And Jesus says reincarnation is false, and that there's one death and after that comes the judgment. His apostles, whom he instructed carefully, reiterated his teachings on this.

Instead Jesus taught about the reality of hell. In fact, he discussed the subject more than anyone else in the Bible.[5]

Luke 12:5 - *But I will warn you whom to fear: fear the One who, after He has killed, <u>has authority to cast into hell</u>; yes, I tell you, fear Him!*

We need to realize that reverence and fear of God is the appropriate response to life. God alone has authority to cast a person into hell. He has the power and authority to decide our fate, therefore we should submit to Him and live our lives the way God would want.

> **John 5:29** - *and will come forth; those who did the good deeds to a resurrection of life, <u>those who committed the evil deeds to a resurrection of judgment</u>.*

What is our orientation to righteousness? Will you enjoy the resurrection to live because you invited Jesus to flow through your life and benefit the people around you? Will you be resurrected to judgment because you clung to your self-centered perspective, looking always and only for what would benefit you?

NOTICE WHAT THE APOSTLES SAY...

The apostles were those who were appointed by the Lord Jesus Christ himself and who were specifically tasked with writing down the truths of the Christian faith and how to live it. These inspired men clearly declare that there is a heaven to gain and a hell to lose.

> **1 Corinthians 6:9-11** - *Or do you not know that <u>the unrighteous will not inherit the kingdom of God?</u> Do not be deceived; neither fornicators, nor idolaters, nor adulterers, nor effeminate, nor homosexuals, nor thieves, nor the covetous, nor drunkards, nor revilers, nor swindlers, will inherit the kingdom of God. <u>Such were some of you; but you were washed, but you were sanctified, but you were justified in the name of the Lord Jesus Christ and in the Spirit of our God.</u>*

The Apostle Paul writes to real people in Corinth who turned their lives around through accepting Jesus as Savior, Lord, and God. They were headed to hell but instead are headed to heaven. He could see their faces and remember the stories of their lives. He warns them about their past friends and those who wandered back to the lifestyle they used to know. God does not produce that kind of fruit. He will not have those things growing in His garden.

Ephesians 5:5 - *For this you know with certainty, that no immoral or impure person or covetous man, who is an idolater, has an inheritance in the kingdom of Christ and God.*

The Apostle Paul tends to state the case in the positive. He emphasizes what sinners will miss out on instead of dwelling on where they are headed if they keep on in their self-centered and sinful ways.

2 Peter 2:4 - *For if God did not spare angels when they sinned, but cast them into hell and committed them to pits of darkness, reserved for judgment*

The Apostle Peter comes right out and declares that angels were assigned to hell and so will people who lead sinful, unrighteous, and self-centered lives. God did not spare angels who are higher on the hierarchical order of beings and therefore He will not spare humans.

NOTICE WHAT VARIOUS OTHER SCRIPTURES SAY...

Throughout the Scriptures God inspired the authors to record the awful nature of hell and the results of an unrighteous life. The testimony about hell shows up in various parts of the Scriptures. Let me show you a few.

Daniel 12:2 - *Many of those who sleep in the dust of the ground will awake, these to everlasting life, but the others to disgrace and everlasting contempt.*

Some who will come to judgment day will be condemned to everlasting contempt. Can you think of people who demonstrated that they pursued self-focused evil? In just the 20th century a few names come to mind:

Adolf Hitler, Joseph Stalin, Rev. Jim Jones, and many others.

Jude 1:6,7 - *And angels who did not keep their own domain, but abandoned their proper abode, <u>He has kept in eternal bonds under darkness for the judgment of the great day</u>,*

Notice the description of hell in this passage. It is eternal bondage. It is darkness and it is waiting for judgment day. In this case Jude is describing the angels who inhabit this place. But he uses their actions to prompt better decisions and actions on the part of his hearers.

Jude 1:12,13 *These are the men who are hidden reefs in your love feasts when they feast with you without fear, caring for themselves; clouds without water, carried along by winds; autumn trees without fruit, doubly dead, uprooted; wild waves of the sea, casting up their own shame like foam; <u>wandering stars, for whom the black darkness has been reserved forever.</u>*

Notice how Jude describes hell for those who disrupt and seek to destroy the church. They will be wandering stars. They will be shut up in black darkness forever because of their choices and actions.

Revelation 21:8 - *But for the cowardly and unbelieving and abominable and murderers and immoral persons and sorcerers and idolaters and all liars, <u>their part will be in the lake that burns with fire and brimstone, which is the second death.</u>*

The second death is separation from the active presence of the grace of God. The imagery is of separation and some type of fire that burns but does not consume.

Revelation 22:15 - *Outside are the dogs and the sorcerers and the immoral persons and the murderers and the idolaters, and everyone who loves and practices lying.*

The lake of fire is postured outside the gates of the heavenly city. The people and angels that are assigned here were excluded from the presence of God; excluded from the joy of life in God; excluded from the significant service given to those inside the city.

Conclusion

What have we learned about why there has to be a hell? We have learned the details of the place called hell. It is a place of awareness of others, consciousness, memories, justice, limits, torment, and flame. It is some type of place that Jesus describes as a temporary holding tank.

We have learned about the architecture of this place called hell and its containment in a larger place called Sheol. We have learned that Sheol has at least two compartments: an upper compartment called Abraham's bosom and a lower compartment called hell. These two compartments house two kinds of people who have gone through a preliminary judgment and then assigned.

We have learned that while at one time those who were righteous were sent at death to this upper compartment called Abraham's bosom to wait until Christ had finally paid for their sins, they now go straight to be with Christ and God the Father in heaven. We have learned that those who remain selfish and rebellious toward God go to a holding tank called hell. We have learned that that holding tank will eventually be emptied into the lake of fire.

As we have poured through the biblical content regarding hell, we have learned at least ten specific things about why there has to be a hell. First, we have learned that the souls of people last forever, therefore, there must be an eternal place for their souls to be. This is either heaven or hell. Have they, through their choices, conformed themselves to the love of God? Hell is the place where the eternal souls of those who have rejected the love of God will exist in an eternal now.

Second, we have learned that there is a need for justice beyond what is accomplished here in this life. Hell is that place where the full measure of justice will be meted out on those who demand to bear the penalties of their own choices. Remember, no one has to pay for their own sins; God offers a way to be forgiven through the work of His Son Jesus Christ.

Third, we have learned that our choices last forever. The things we decide to do and not do will echo through our lives, our family's lives, and into eternity.

Fourth, we have learned that selfishness continues to grow even after death. While the physical body of a person may cease to function, their soul continues to produce more of what they were already producing -- an eternity of growing selfishness that needs to be warehoused.

Fifth, we have learned that the sinfulness of mankind and the angels needs to be contained so that it does not contaminate eternity. Hell is that container that quarantines the mountains of growing rebellion and selfishness in mankind and fallen angels.

Sixth, we have learned that sin has much further impact than any of us have been led to believe. The butterfly effects of sin is what will allow us to embrace the need for sin and the souls of those who still cling to their sin to be contained in the lake of fire.

Seventh, we learned that while humanity may have shifting definitions of what is right and wrong based upon culture and emotional reactions to familiar actions, God is omniscient and immutable. He knows what is really right and good for people and what is not. He does not change

His mind about what will benefit the individual, the family, and the society because He really knows.

Eighth, we have learned that there is a hierarchy of beings. Some beings are more valuable than others, and it follows that the Supreme Being is the most valuable. Any offense against Him is more heinous than other sins against lesser beings.

Ninth, we learned that everyone has a point of no return in terms of their attitude to righteousness. Once a person reaches and passes that point of no return, that person will not change no matter how much grace is offered.

Tenth, we have learned that all the Christian experts and God Himself tell us that there will be hell and a lake of fire. Jesus, Paul, Daniel, John, Peter, and numerous other witnesses in Scripture declare that hell is real and can be avoided.

What are we to say in conclusion about this place of ultimate justice and containment of selfishness, wickedness, and sin? Yes, there is a hell that contains the eternal souls of people who have rejected the way of God. They have rejected God's forgiveness, and God will not impose even His forgiveness upon people who do not want it. Hell exists. It is real, even though we might wish that it were not.

God is searching for those who will choose to love Him and worship Him (John 4:24). He does not force anyone to follow Him, but He does strongly invite people to give their life to Him (John 6:44; Hebrews 3:7). God, because He loved us, has offered us a way to escape the justice, punishment, and torment of hell. He knew that we would need to have a way of escape for sinful humanity. From before He created the universe He had a perfect plan to allow people to escape the fires of hell. His plan was His only begotten Son. God sent His only begotten Son to the earth to live a perfect life and then voluntarily give up that life as a substitute for each of us and our sins and wicked choices (John 3:16; Romans 5:8-10). He told us that if we believed in Him as our Savior that He would rescue us from this awful place called hell (John 6:29). He would also enter into our lives and teach us how to live lives of peace and joy in the Holy Spirit (Romans 14:17).

If you would like to formally invite Jesus Christ to be your Savior so that you can escape an afterlife in hell, pray this prayer:

Dear Lord Jesus,

I know that I am a sinner and deserve the fires of hell for my selfishness, sin, and mistakes. I want to turn my life around. The only way I can do that is to have You (Jesus) come run my life and be my Savior. I turn over the control of my life to You (Jesus) and ask that you would save me and make me the kind of person you want me to be.

In the name of the Lord Jesus Christ,

Amen

Let us look at the powerful integration of God's offer of heaven and the truth of hell at the end of the Bible in Revelation 22:12-17:

> **Revelation 22:12-17** - *Behold, I am coming quickly, and My reward is with Me, to render to every man according to what he has done. I am the Alpha and the Omega, the first and the last, the beginning and the end. Blessed are those who wash their robes, so that they may have the right to the tree of life, and may enter by the*

Conclusion

gates into the city. Outside <u>are</u> the dogs and the sorcerers and the immoral persons and the murderers and the idolaters, and everyone <u>who loves and practices lying</u>. I, Jesus, have sent My angel to testify to you these things for the churches. I am the root and the descendant of David, the bright morning star. The Spirit and the bride say, "Come." And let the one who hears say, "Come." And let the one who is thirsty come; let the one who wishes take the water of life without cost.

Notice that Jesus, through His angelic messenger, reemphasizes the reality of hell and its eternal nature. But the bulk of His message is that a way has been made to offer forgiveness and access to the heavenly city. Access to God is available. No one has to end up in hell, the lake of fire, or outside of the blessing of God.

The forgiveness of God awaits in the sacrifice of Jesus Christ on your behalf. Accept Christ and avoid the justice of hell.

End Notes

Preface

1. Wells, Jonathan, *Icons of Evolution*, Regnery Publishing; First Edition, First Trade Paper Edition, January 2002.

Chapter 1

1. Moreland, J.P., quoted in *The Case for Faith* by Lee Strobel, Zondervan, Grand Rapids, Michigan, 49530, 2000, 171

2. ibid, 173

Chapter 2

1. Chesterton, G.K., quoted in *The Case for Faith* by Lee Strobel, Zondervan, Grand Rapids, Michigan, 49530, 2000 169

Chapter 3

1. Turner, Alice, *The History of Hell*, Harcourt Brace & Company, 8th floor, Orlando, Fl 32887 quoting David Lodge, "How far can you go"

2. Turner, Alice, *The History of Hell*, 3

Chapter 4

1. Moreland, J.P., quoted in *The Case for Faith* by Lee Strobel, 174

2. Turner, Alice, *The History of Hell*, 1

3. Moreland, J.P., quoted in *The Case for Faith* by Lee Strobel, 174

4. ibid, 175

5. ibid, 178

6. ibid, 177

7. ibid, 192

8. Carson, D.A., quoted in *The Case for Faith* by Lee Strobel, Zondervan, Grand Rapids, Michigan, 49530, 2000, 193

Chapter 5

1. Moreland, J.P., quoted in *The Case for Faith* by Lee Strobel, 173

2. ibid, 187

3. ibid, 180

4. Milton's *Paradise Lost* quoted in the *History of Hell* by Alice Turner, 180

5. Moreland, J.P., quoted in *The Case for Faith* by Lee Strobel, 190

Appendix 1
The Disciplines of Repetition
Biblical Meditation

We have done a fairly extensive look at three sections of Scripture, but it is always helpful to meditate on the biblical verses yourself. Therefore I have included this overview of the techniques of biblical meditation and the blank meditation worksheets to allow you to ruminate over these passages yourself. I have included ten blank sheets so that you can try all the various biblical techniques on each passage. I can remember my youth pastor always wanting ten pages of biblical meditation worksheets. He wanted me to press the Scriptures through every part of who I was: my spirit, my mind, my will, my emotions, and even my body. You never know which of the techniques will unlock an insight, a connection to God, a new application.

People are talking about meditation these days as though it were the sole property of the Eastern religions. Eastern religions practice a form of meditation. Using broad general categories, there are two types of meditation: **Emptying forms** of meditation and **content-based forms** of meditation. All meditation is the focused attention of the mind upon something. In emptying forms of meditation the mind is focused on a nonsense idea, word, phrase, or a logical absurdity in order to attempt an escape from the present space-time logical constraints. In content-based meditation the mind is focused on some form of content. There are three forms of content-based meditation: materialistic, spiritual and biblical. Biblical meditation is "content-based" meditation with biblical words, ideas, phrases, and precepts as the meditated content. The new biblical qualities, reactions, and ideas will become a part of the person who is being shaped into Christ-likeness. The goal of the Christian is to have the Lord's thoughts become their thoughts (Isaiah 55:6-8; Psalm 1:1-3; Colossians 3:16; Joshua 1:8; Philippians 4:8; Deuteronomy 6:6-9).

The Incredible Power of Biblical Meditation

The most powerful form of transformational life-change known to man is meditation. In fact, no long-term life-change can take place without this meditation. The tragedy in Christian circles is that this powerful method is often unknown, unused, and in some cases even reviled. Biblical meditation was common practice in the Christian church for 1900 years. Yet in the last 150 years biblical meditation has been left behind in the modern church as it searches for newer programs and crowd-pleasing techniques. The prophet Amos tells of a time when there will be a famine in the land: *Not a famine for bread, or a thirst for water, but rather for hearing the words of the Lord.* (Amos 8:11) We are living out a fulfillment of that vision. More Bibles are printed than ever before and yet the power of the Bible is not connecting with the souls of God's people. All the power people want for transformational life-change is near but remains untapped.

What is Biblical Meditation?

The idea behind biblical meditation is taken from a sheep or cow chewing its cud. The animal chews the grass and works it into a mush and then swallows it. It then brings it back up later to chew it some more. It repeats this process until all the nutrients have been extracted from the grass. Meditation is murmuring or repeating the concepts, ideas, and words of Scripture to extract all the richness and wisdom.

Biblical meditation is referred to in a number of ways in the Scriptures: delighting in Scripture (Psalm 119:16, 34, 47, 70); delighting in the Lord (Psalm 37:4); letting the Word of God richly dwell in your soul (Colossians 3:16); setting your mind on things above (Colossians 3:1); setting your mind on the Spirit (Romans 8:6); renewing your mind (Romans 12:2).

What Are the Techniques of Biblical Meditation?

Down through the centuries of Judeo-Christian history strong believers have discovered a number of methods for "chewing" Scripture. These techniques move the believer significantly forward in their pursuit of God and attainment of Christ-like living. The following list is not meant to be exhaustive or prioritized. Some will find certain techniques more helpful than others.

Confessionalize Scripture

To confessionalize Scripture is to take the Bible through your will. It is the process of comparing your life with the biblical standard and asking God whether this is true of your life. Every phrase or sentence of Scripture forms a way of examining your life.

First, each truth or action exposed in that Scripture is confessed as true and important. "Dear Lord, I agree with you that Christians should love one another."

Second, each truth or action is confessed as something you are doing or something that you are not doing. "Dear Lord, I freely admit that I am having a very difficult time loving this person right now. I know that I should, but I do not. Create in me a heart of love for this person." Or, "Dear Lord, I am encouraged to say that I am acting in a loving way toward my wife. I thank you for teaching me how to love her." Specifically and openly comparing your life with Scripture is a powerful way to draw the Bible through your will.

Visualize Scripture

The idea of biblical mediation through visualization is to take a passage of Scripture and make it come to life in your mind. It can be referred to as making a mental picture or movie of a biblical scene or concept. For thousands of years all societies have declared the power of the mind to shape behavior and achievement. There are at least two kinds of Scripture to visualize: narrative and didactic.

Narrative visualization is where one sees a biblical story actually taking place. Smelling the smells; hearing the sounds around the event; touching the equipment or clothing of the individuals in the story. In narrative meditation there needs to be focused attention on the biblical detail and an educated imagination to fill out the narrative story line.

The second type of visualization is **didactic visualization.** This is where one pictures the truth of Scripture being lived out in present reality. When this is applied to doctrinal aspects of Scripture, the doctrinal truths are pictured. One might recognize the unseen hand of God moving on, in, and through the men who penned the Scripture to keep it error free and accurate. When this is applied to a practical principle for living, the principle is viewed as being lived out in life, such as being gentle in response to a sarcastic remark as in Proverbs 15:1. The key idea here is to actually picture oneself living out a scriptural concept. What has to be done to get in a position to live this biblical idea? If you can't see yourself doing a righteous idea in your mind, you will never do it. You have to see it before you will do it.

One of the clearest examples of this type of meditation is in Colossians 3:1-14. The apostle orders Christians to "set their minds on the things above;" "Put to death your earthly members: fornication, impurity, etc;" "Put on a heart of compassion, kindness, humility..." Each of these commands is a mental exercise designed to cause you to "see" what is not your present experience. We are to see ourselves enjoying the wonders of heaven, intimacy with God, the qualities of Christ, entering into the heavenly economy, etc. We are to picture ourselves as unresponsive and unaffected by those temptations that are the most powerful in our lives. We are to make a mental movie of the qualities of Christ being our normal lifestyle. Mental movie-making of biblical ideas is God's way of renewing our minds.

Personalize Scripture

Personalizing Scripture can bring the power of an individual Scripture directly into your emotions. This technique is accomplished by inserting your name or a personal pronoun into a verse when saying it. One of the reasons that the Psalms are such a popular section of the Scripture is that in many cases they are already personalized. Years ago I was counseling a woman who was really having a hard time staying in her marriage. She wanted to end her marriage and pursue her selfish desires.

I asked her to pray and ask God what she should do. She began praying and God began to bring back into her mind the Scriptural directions for wives in Ephesians 5 with her name woven through the commands. This was immensely powerful. "God spoke to me," she said. "He spoke to me and I will never forget it." This time of prayerful meditation was a turning point in her life. She went back home and threw herself into her marriage with new hope and determination. Her marriage improved dramatically because God had spoken through Scripture as it was being personalized to her.

Record Insights

Usually during the time when you are using the other methods of biblical meditation you will become aware of ancillary questions, insights, connections, or bits of wisdom that are in some ways connected to the Scripture but may not be the main points of the passage. These are called insights. It is as though God begins to open the Scriptures to you and the levels of wisdom contained within it. Christians have usually found that if they write down insights as they are meditating, then they receive more of these insights. It is almost like saying to God, "I'm paying attention." Sometimes this is called spiritual journaling. A meditation journal is a helpful way of recording your reactions, thoughts, insights, and promptings during meditation.

Pray Scripture

This technique is to turn the actual phrases of Scripture into prayers. It is very educational to pray God's desires back to Him. As your mind seeks ways to turn various passages into requests you will uncover new angles and depth of understanding on the will of God. In every passage there are many different ways to turn the truths into prayer requests. This type of prayer resembles the Apostle Paul's prayers in Ephesians 1:18-21 and Ephesians 3:14-21. Asking for scriptural realities is often the best kind of praying for it keeps us from asking from a limited materialistic perspective. When we verbalize what God wants us to desire, we see the stark contrast between God's desires for us and our own fleshly desires.

Harmonize

There are at least two ways to meditate on Scripture through song. One is to sing the actual words of Scripture and adjust the tune to work with the unaltered words of the biblical text. The second method for meditating on Scripture through song is to take the truths, ideas, or concepts of the Scripture and sing those. This is a little easier and more free-flowing. When singing the Scripture it does not matter if it is great music, just that you are expressing the truths, feelings, and desires of Scripture. You will laugh, smile, ponder, and re-commit to the Lord as you sing the words or concepts of Scripture. It is really an enjoyable process, but it takes a little courage to get started.

Open the Bible, pick a tune you know, and begin singing the words of Scripture to the tune. Another way to harmonize the Scripture is to look at a passage or a Christian doctrine and write down three or four truths. Start making up a song about those truths. The tune and the words are changeable as long as they accurately reflect the truth of Scripture. Many of our great hymns and gospel songs have come from just such meditations. The writers were not trying to write great hymns but to express their heart and soul regarding the truths of God. "Amazing Grace" by John Newton, "Amazing Love" by

Charles Wesley, and various versions of the Apostles Creed that have been set to music are all examples of this type of meditation.

What Are the Results of Biblical Meditation?
God makes some amazing promises in the Scripture regarding biblical meditation. In Joshua 1:8 and Psalm 1:1-3 God promises believers if they meditate on His law, they will be prosperous and successful. The mind filled with biblical principles and laws will avoid many of the hidden reefs that sink other people's lives. When a Christian purposefully fills their mind with Scripture, then the God of peace will move in and reassure that person that He is still in charge and He has a way through every storm (Colossians 3:16). In Psalm 119:97-100, God promises believers that they will gain wisdom beyond their years if they meditate upon biblical concepts.

When Are the Best Times to Meditate?
God has specifically suggested particular times to ruminate on Scripture (Deuteronomy 6:6-9; Psalm 1:1-3; 4:4; 63:6). **First**, the Scripture says to meditate when we sit in our homes. This means that one must turn off the TV at times. Many business travelers would lessen the temptations of travel and increase intimacy with God by turning off the television when they travel. **Second**, the Scripture suggests that people should get into the habit of reorienting their minds to Scripture as they are going from place to place. This is a time to pre-plan the next appointment using biblical concepts and qualities. A **third** time to meditate on Scripture is right before going to sleep. As people focus their minds on the concepts, qualities, and words of Scripture right before they drift off to sleep, it allows their subconscious mind to embrace these concepts.

A **fourth** time to meditate each day is when the day begins. Many Christians set aside time each morning to spend extended time with God through biblical meditation. A **fifth** time for meditation is the night watches. These are times in the middle of the night spent with God and His Word.

The Disciplines of Repetition: Conclusion

Memorization and meditation are not the only disciplines of repetition, but they have for centuries formed two of the more crucial practices that develop the spiritual Christian. It is not enough merely to understand these practices; one must actually do them on a regular basis to impact the depths of the soul. The goal of memorization and meditation is to give God the Holy Spirit an ever-increasing supply of language and concepts to use when communicating with us. A third discipline of repetition is teaching. To use teaching as a discipline of repetition is to seek to explain what God has taught you. You don't have to be teacher and have gifts of teaching to teach. You just need to want to pass on the truths of the faith to others and in this way it will cement the truth to your own mind. My hope is that you will take the materials in this book and teach others in small groups, one on one and the like.

Journal of Biblical Meditation

Scripture	
Slow Repetition	
Memorization	
Study	
Personalize	
Confessing	
Praying	
Envisioning	
Singing	
Journal Insights	
Diagramming/ Analogy	
Personal Translation	

Journal of Biblical Meditation

Scripture	
Slow Repetition	
Memorization	
Study	
Personalize	
Confessing	
Praying	
Envisioning	
Singing	
Journal Insights	
Diagramming/ Analogy	
Personal Translation	

Journal of Biblical Meditation

Scripture	
Slow Repetition	
Memorization	
Study	
Personalize	
Confessing	
Praying	
Envisioning	
Singing	
Journal Insights	
Diagramming/ Analogy	
Personal Translation	

About The Author

Gil Stieglitz is a catalyst for positive change both personally and organizationally. He excites, educates, and motivates audiences all over the world through passion, humor, leadership, and wisdom. He has led seminars in China, Europe, Canada, Mexico, and all over the United States.

In 1992, Dr. Gil founded the non-profit ministry *Principles to Live By* to help people and organizations win at life through biblical wisdom. Dr. Gil has been asked to repair, lead, and reinvigorate numerous organizations and individuals. He successfully led a church to 1,400% growth in a disadvantaged area. As a Denominational Superintendent in the Western United States, he led 50 churches and 250 pastors to over 300% growth. As a Superintendent of Schools, he oversaw a school system as it doubled in four years. As an executive pastor at a megachurch, he rebuilt a staff and added over one thousand people to its congregation. He injects dynamic life-change as a professor at universities and graduate schools on the West Coast and through seminars, sermons, and lecture series. He also partners with Courage Worldwide, a ministry that rescues young girls away from forced sexual slavery in America.

He has a B.A. from Biola University, as well as a Master's Degree and a Doctorate in Christian Leadership from Talbot School of Theology. He has authored over two- dozen books, manuals, and development courses including three best sellers. Dr. Gil's resources are available at Amazon.com as well as at www.ptlb.com.

Gil and his wife, Dana, have enjoyed over twenty-five years of marriage and reside in Roseville, California, where they raised their three precious girls.

Other Resources by Gil Stieglitz

Books

Becoming Courageous

Breakfast with Solomon Volume 1

Breakfast with Solomon Volume 2

Breakfast with Solomon Volume 3

Breaking Satanic Bondage

Deep Happiness: The Eight Secrets

Delighting in God

Delighting in Jesus

Developing a Christian Worldview

God's Radical Plan for Husbands

God's Radical Plan for Wives

Going Deep In Prayer: 40 Days of In-Depth Prayer

Leading a Thriving Ministry

Marital Intelligence

Mission Possible: Winning the Battle Over Temptation

Proverbs: A Devotional Commentary Volume 1

Proverbs: A Devotional Commentary Volume 2

Satan and The Origin of Sin

Secrets of God's Armor

Spiritual Disciplines of a C.H.R.I.S.T.I.A.N.

They Laughed When I Wrote Another Book About Prayer, Then They Read It

Touching the Face of God: 40 Days of Adoring God

Why There Has to Be a Hell

Podcasts

Becoming a Godly Parent

Biblical Meditation: The Keys of Transformation

Everyday Spiritual Warfare Series

God's Guide to Handling Money

Spiritual War Surrounding Money

The Four Keys to a Great Family

The Ten Commandments

If you would be interested in having Gil Stieglitz speak to your group, you can contact him through the website, www.ptlb.com.

www.ingramcontent.com/pod-product-compliance
Lightning Source LLC
LaVergne TN
LVHW041623070426
835507LV00008B/429